This book belongs to:

____

given this ___ day of

_____________________, 20___

by:

____

I hope you will enjoy coloring
all the pages in this book.
Although the artwork was designed
with adults in mind,
it is appropriate for all ages.
The designs are single-sided
to prevent any bleed-through from one page
from spoiling the artwork on the next.
Feel free to use the reverse sides
for notes or doodling,
or you may choose to leave them blank.
Enjoy!

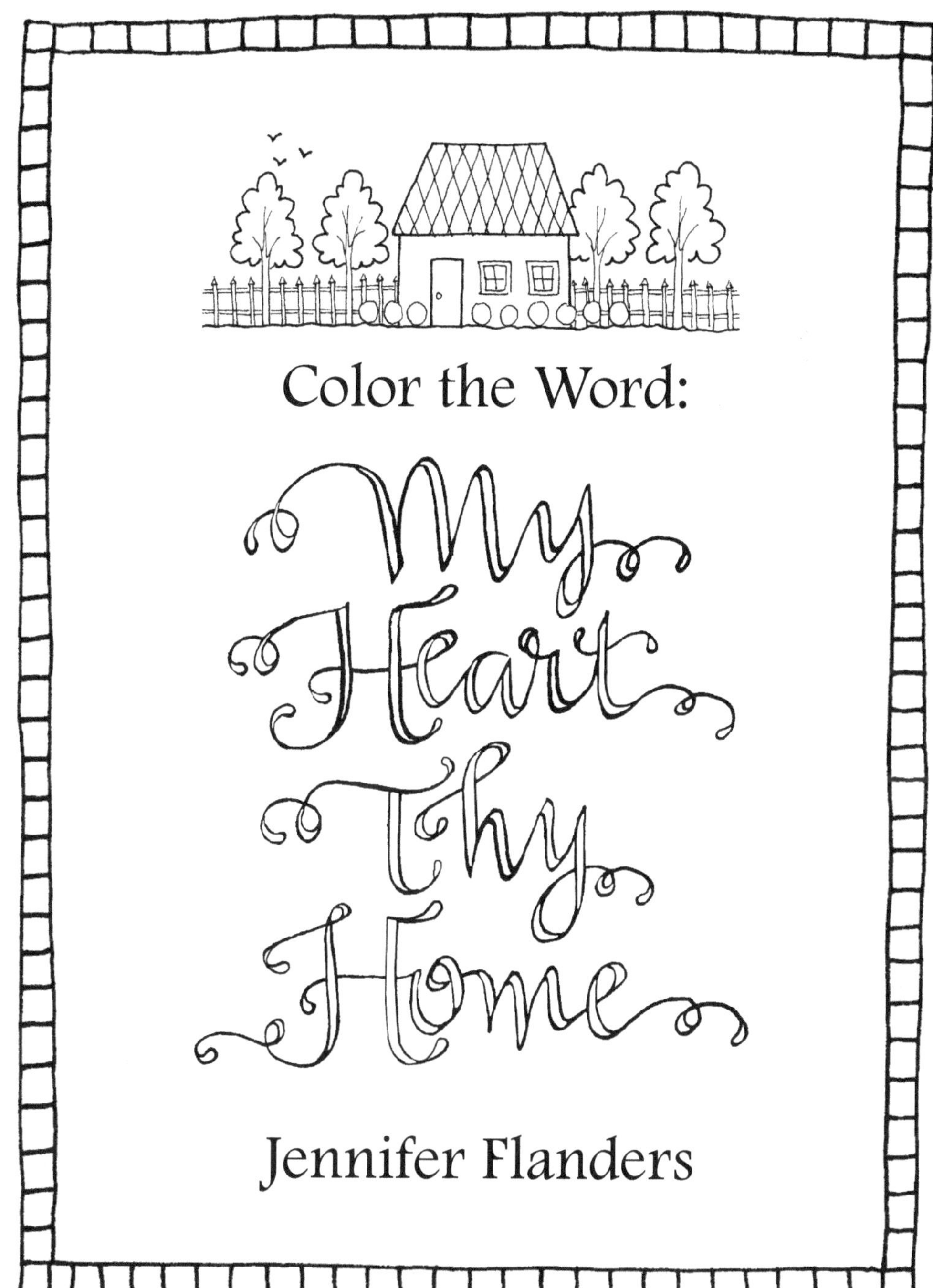

Color the Word:

My Heart Thy Home

Jennifer Flanders

Prescott Publishing

All Scripture references in this book have been taken from one of the following sources:

- The authorized version of *The King James Holy Bible*.
- *God's Word® Translation* of the Holy Bible, © 1995 by God's Word to the Nations. Used by permission of Baker Publishing Group.
- *The English Standard Bible®*. Copyright © 2001 by Crossway Bibles, a publishing ministry of Good News Publishers..
- *The New International Version* of the Holy Bible ®. Copyright ©1973, 1978, 1984 by International Bible Society.
- *The New King James Bible*, ©1982, by Thomas Nelson, Inc.
- *The New Living Bible*, ©1996, 2004. Used by permission of Tyndale House Publishers, Inc. Wheaton, IL 60189. All rights reserved.
- *The New American Standard Bible®*, Copyright ©1960, 1962, 1963, 1968, 1971, 1972, 1973, 1975, 1977, 1995 by the Lockman Foundation. Used by permission.
- *The NET (New English Translation) Bible*©1996-2006, by Biblical Studies Press, L.L.C. http://netbible.com. Used with permission. All rights reserved.

All artwork in this book has been taken from one of the following sources:

- Original designs, hand-drawn and/or hand-lettered by the author, and then scanned into the text.
- A *Masterclips 101,000 Premium Images Collection* that the author's husband bought her back in 1996, long before she ever started blogging or writing or publishing anything, just because "it was on sale for a great price and seemed like something she might like."
- The Graphics Fairy (*thegraphicsfairy.com*), which is a great online source of free vintage clipart. Additional images (and permission to use them in this publication) were obtained by joining her premium membership site (*members.thegraphicsfairy.com*).
- A website called Open Clip Art (*openclipart.org*), which specializes in public domain images.

ISBN: 978-1-938945-19-9

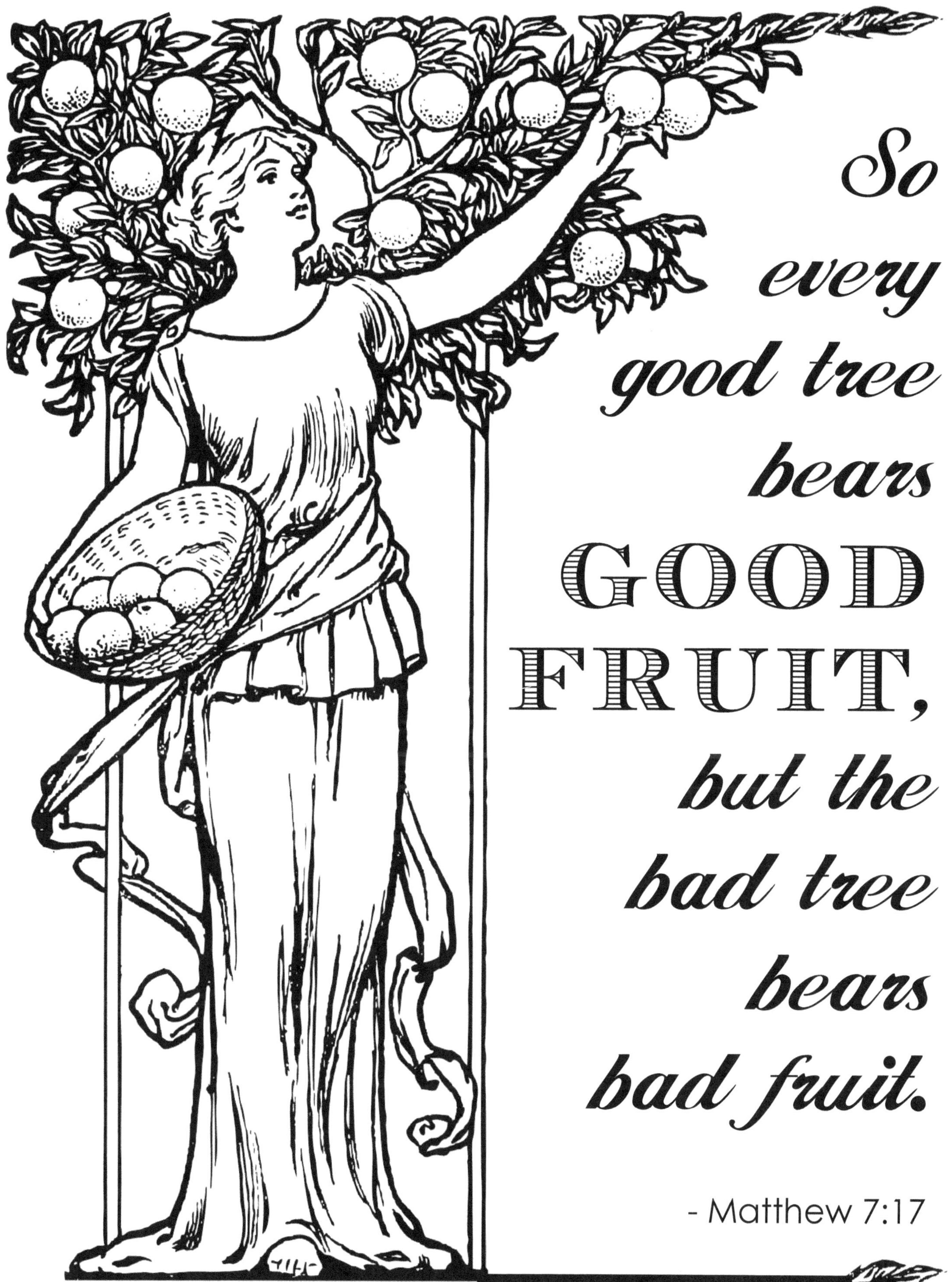
So
every
good tree
bears
GOOD
FRUIT,
but the
bad tree
bears
bad fruit.
- Matthew 7:17

All Scripture is inspired
by God and profitable
for teaching, for reproof,
for correction, and
for training in righteousness.

- 2 Timothy 3:16

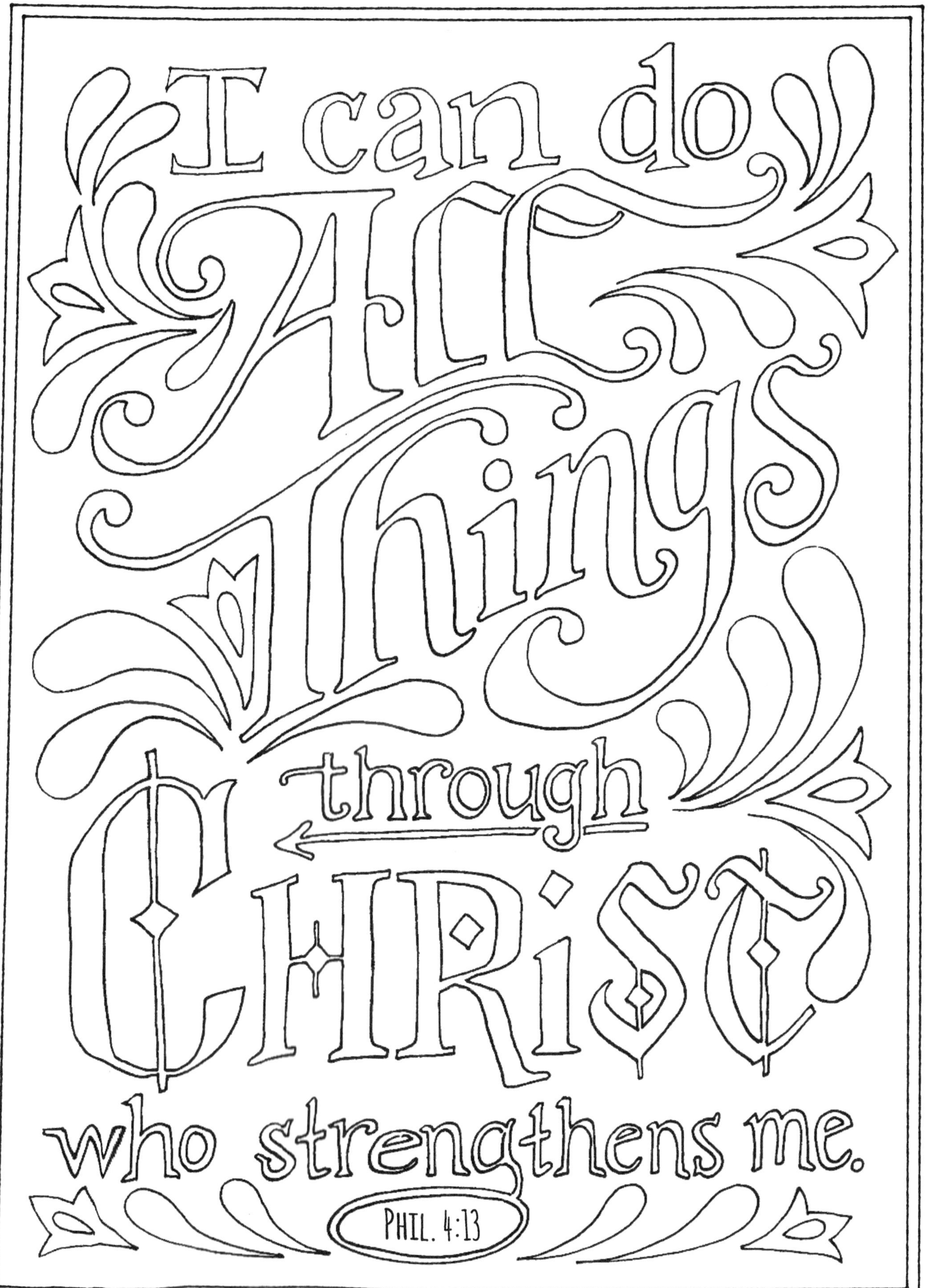
I can do
All
Things
through
CHRIST
who strengthens me.
PHIL. 4:13

All Scripture is inspired
by God and profitable
for teaching, for reproof,
for correction, and
for training in righteousness.

-2 Timothy 3:16

TEACH US TO NUMBER OUR

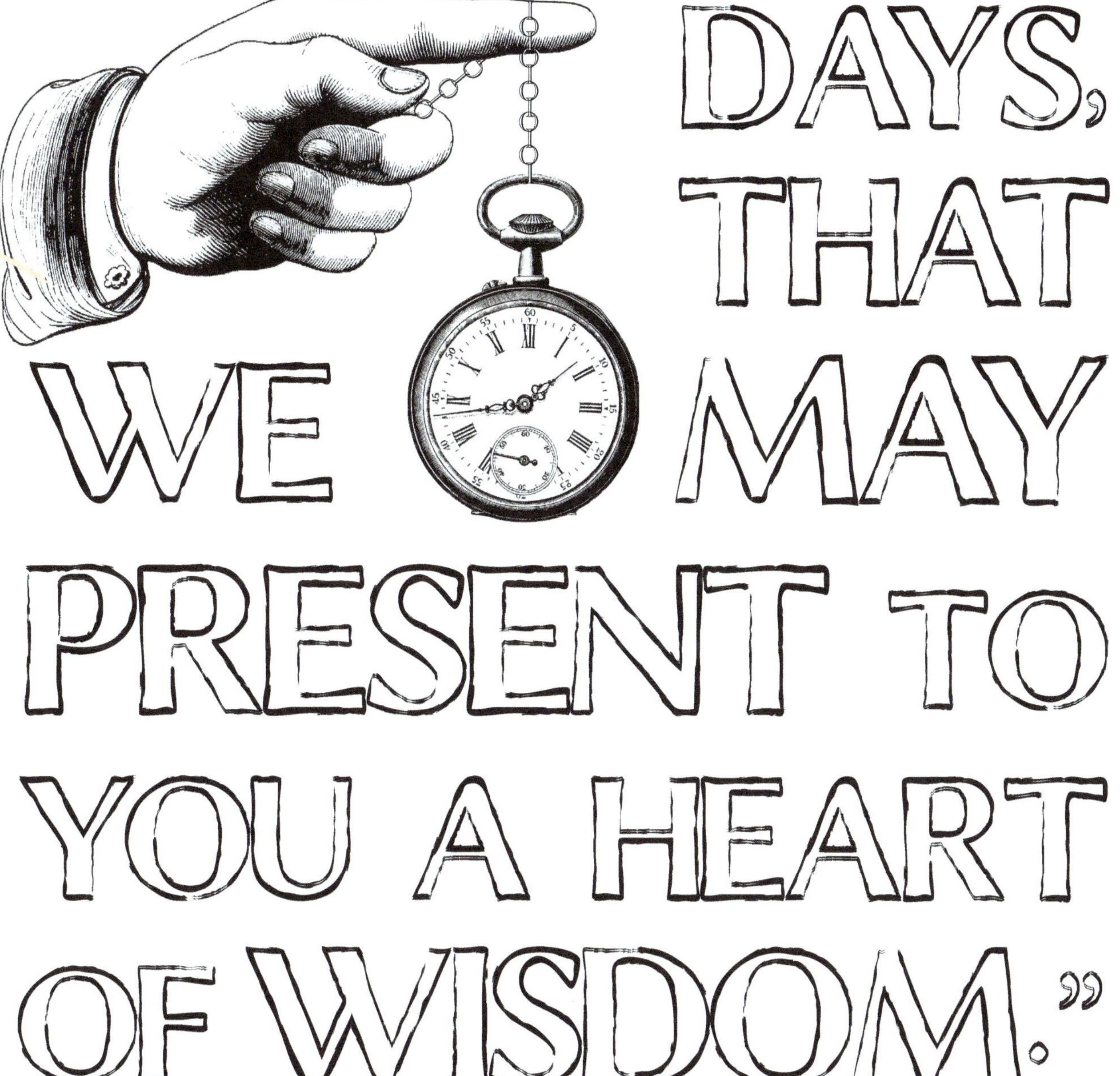

DAYS, THAT WE MAY PRESENT TO YOU A HEART OF WISDOM."

- Psalm 90:12

All Scripture is inspired
by God and profitable
for teaching, for reproof,
for correction, and
for training in righteousness.

- 2 Timothy 3:16

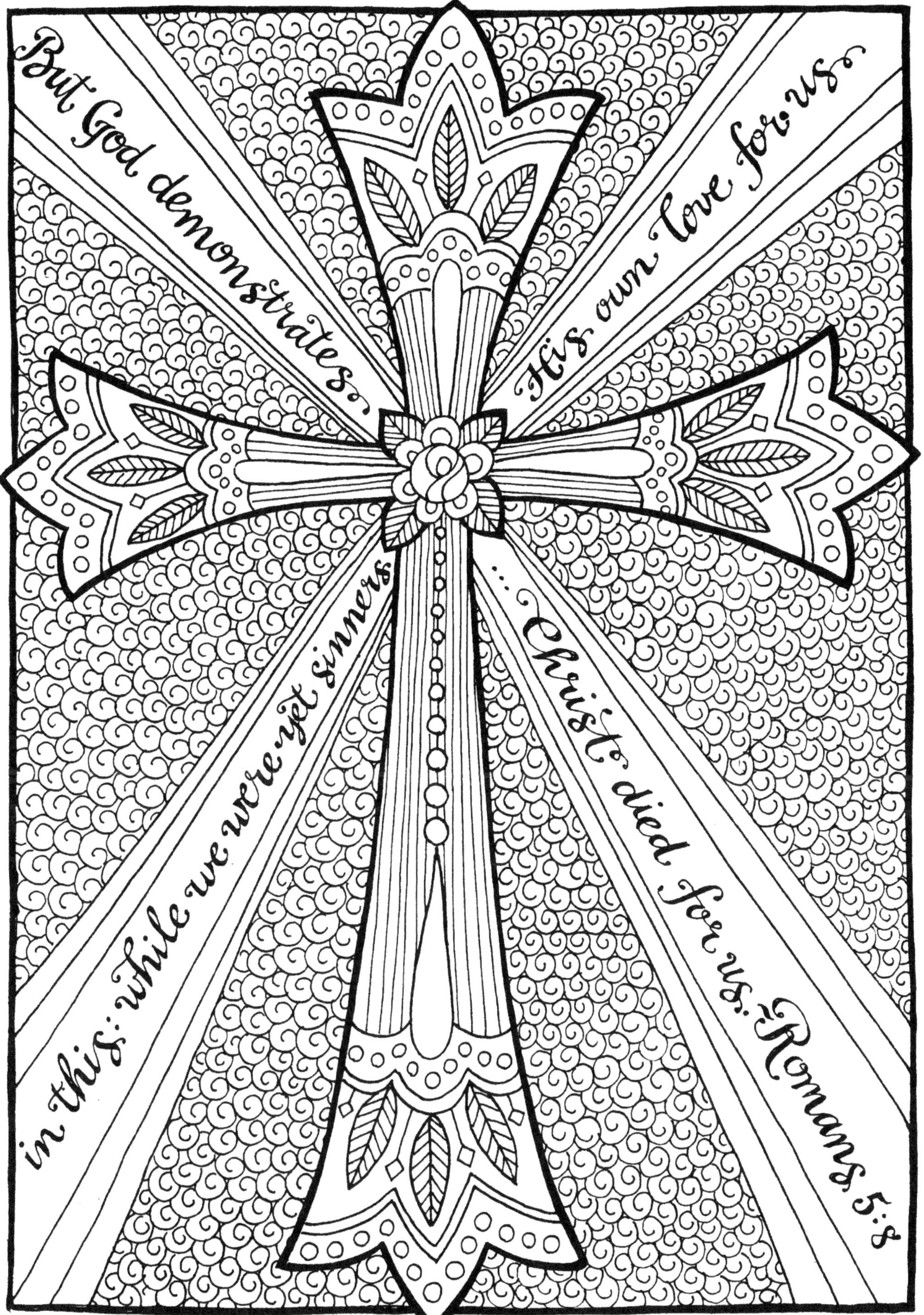
But God demonstrates
His own love for us
in this: while we were yet sinners,
...Christ died for us. Romans 5:8

All Scripture is inspired
by God and profitable
for teaching, for reproof,
for correction, and
for training in righteousness.

- 2 Timothy 3:16

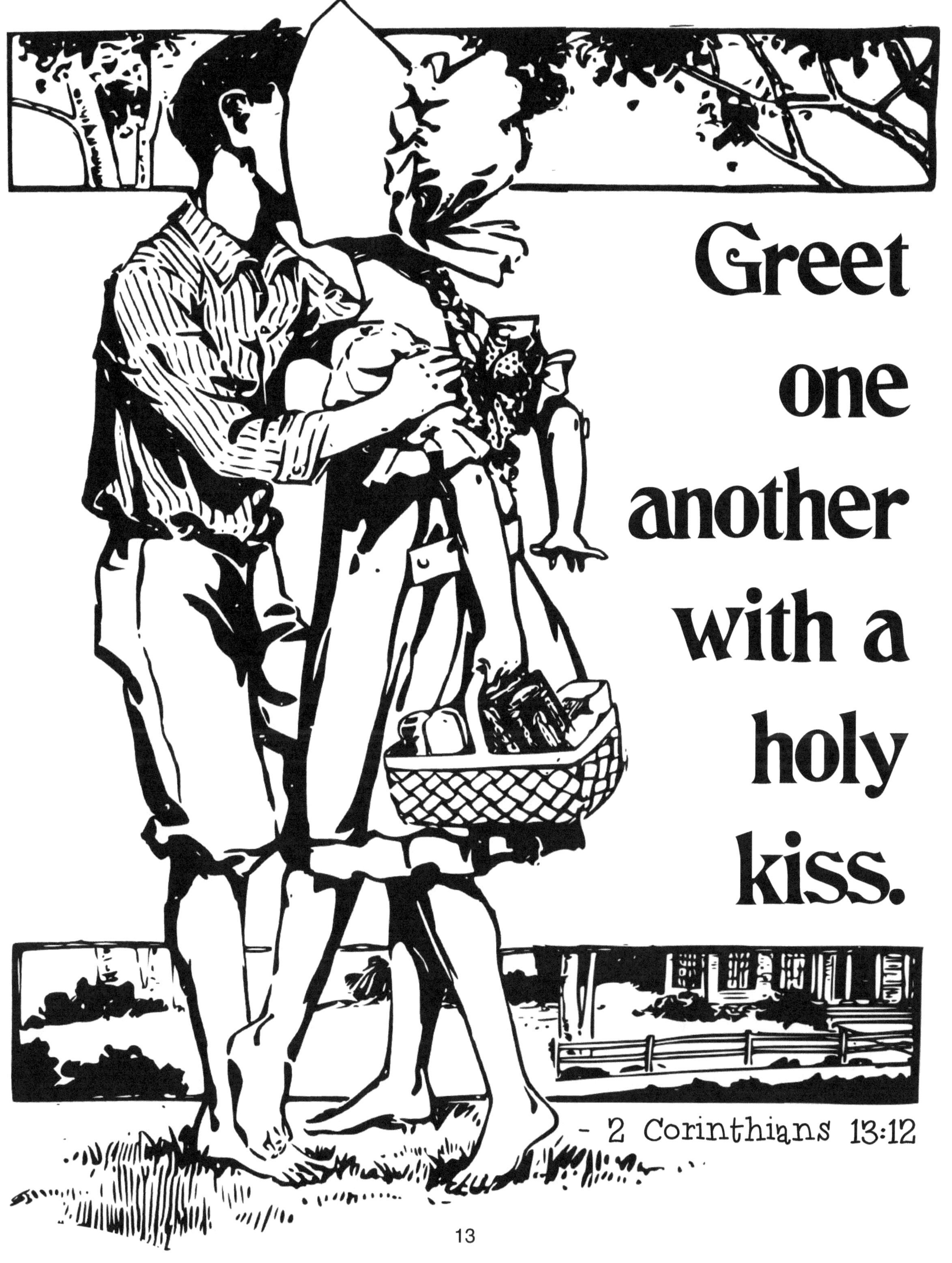
Greet
one
another
with a
holy
kiss.
- 2 Corinthians 13:12

All Scripture is inspired
by God and profitable
for teaching, for reproof,
for correction, and
for training in righteousness.

– 2 Timothy 3:16

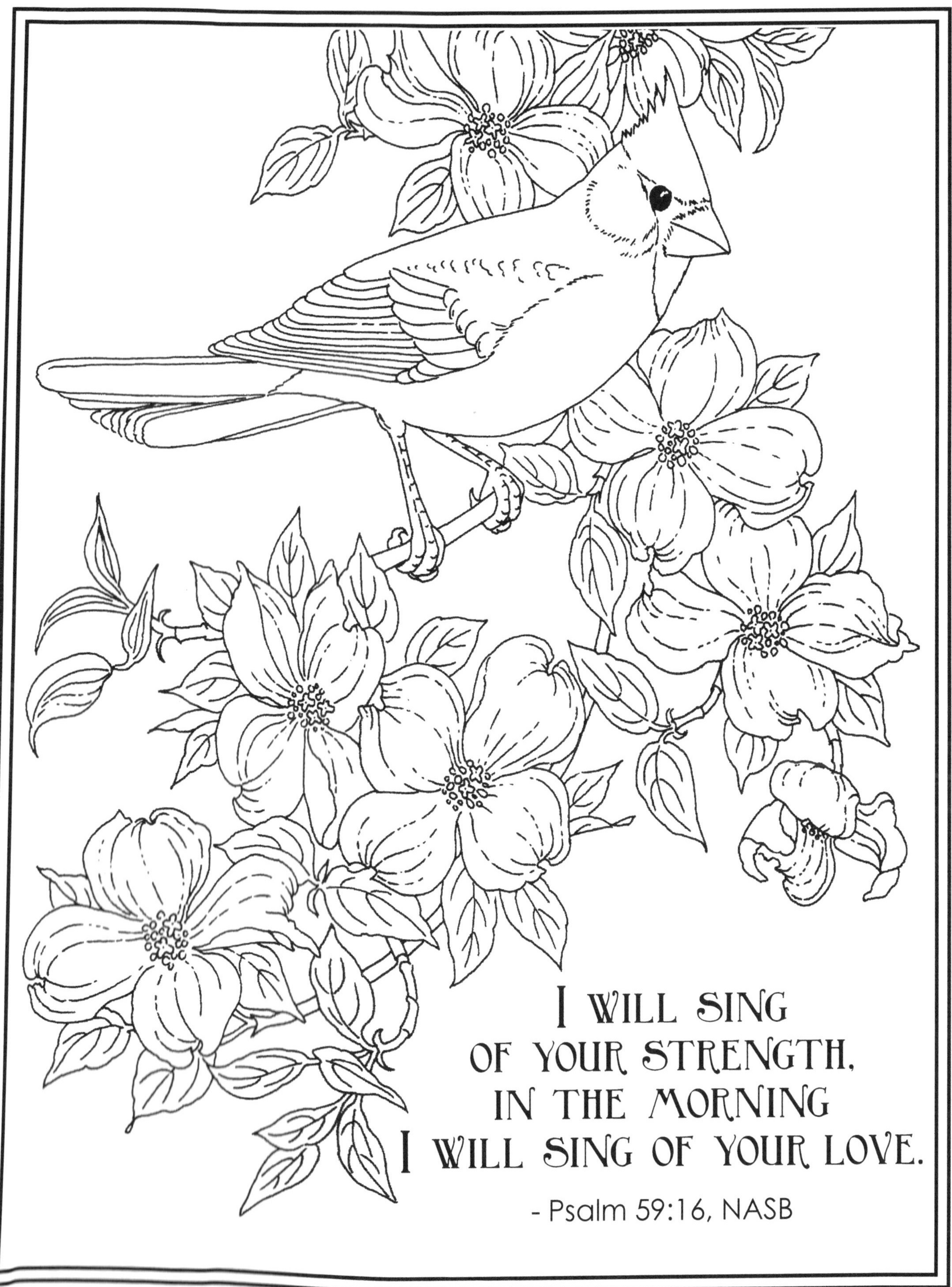
I WILL SING
OF YOUR STRENGTH,
IN THE MORNING
I WILL SING OF YOUR LOVE.
- Psalm 59:16, NASB

All Scripture is inspired
by God and profitable
for teaching, for reproof,
for correction, and
for training in righteousness.

- 2 Timothy 3:16

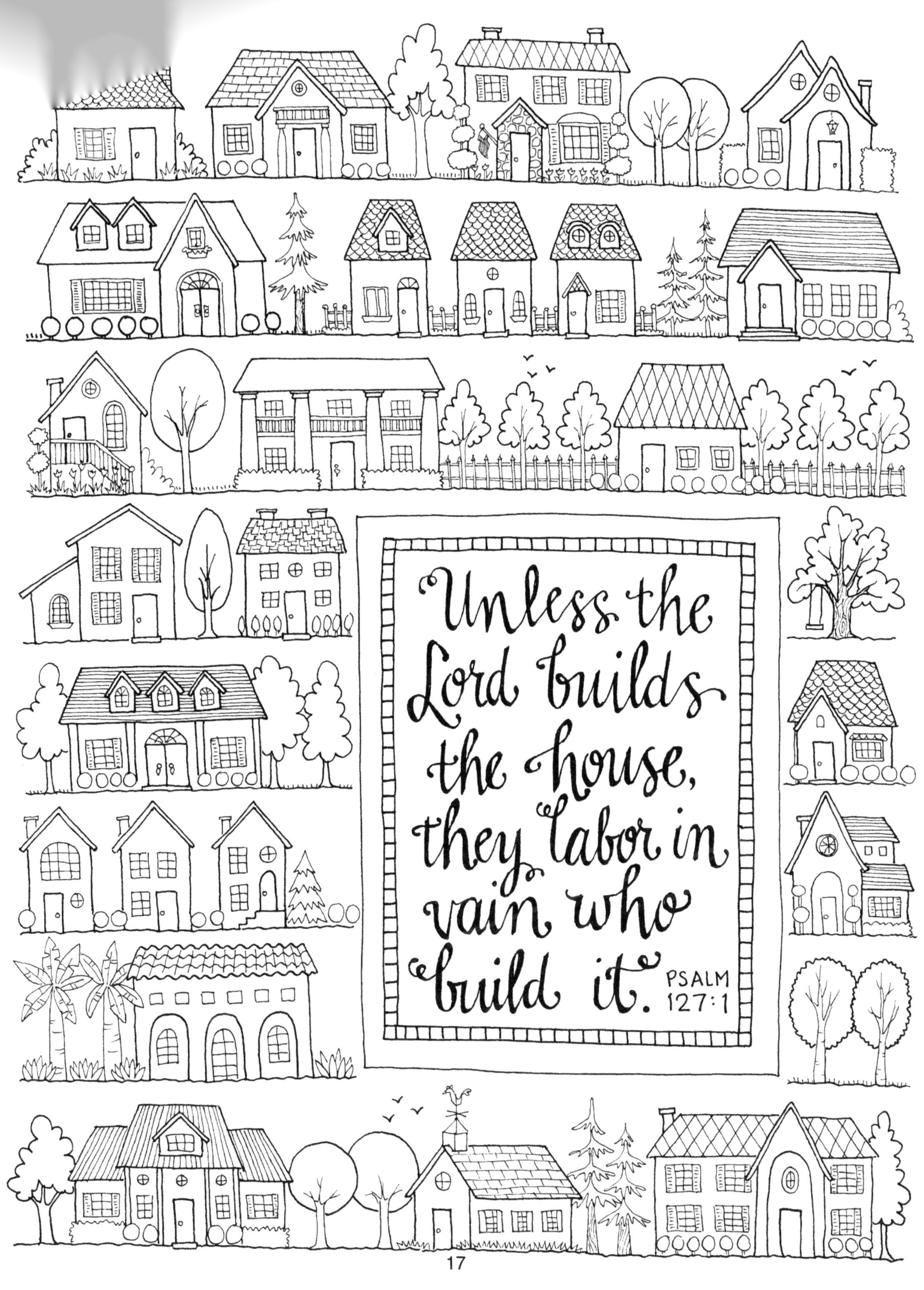
Unless the Lord builds the house, they labor in vain who build it.
PSALM 127:1

All Scripture is inspired
by God and profitable
for teaching, for reproof,
for correction, and
for training in righteousness.

- 2 Timothy 3:16

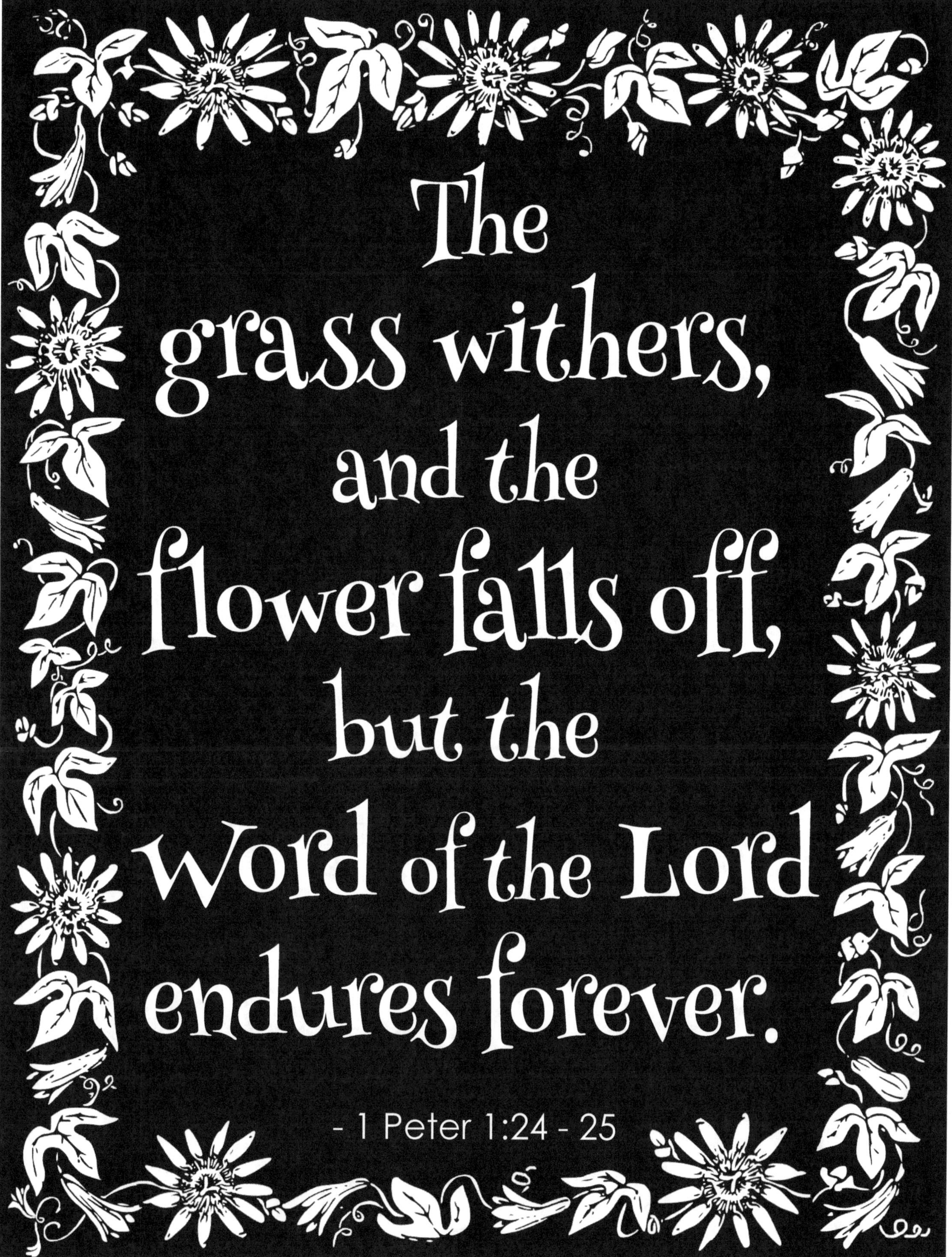
The
grass withers,
and the
flower falls off,
but the
Word of the Lord
endures forever.
- 1 Peter 1:24 - 25

All Scripture is inspired
by God and profitable
for teaching, for reproof,
for correction, and
for training in righteousness.

- 2 Timothy 3:16

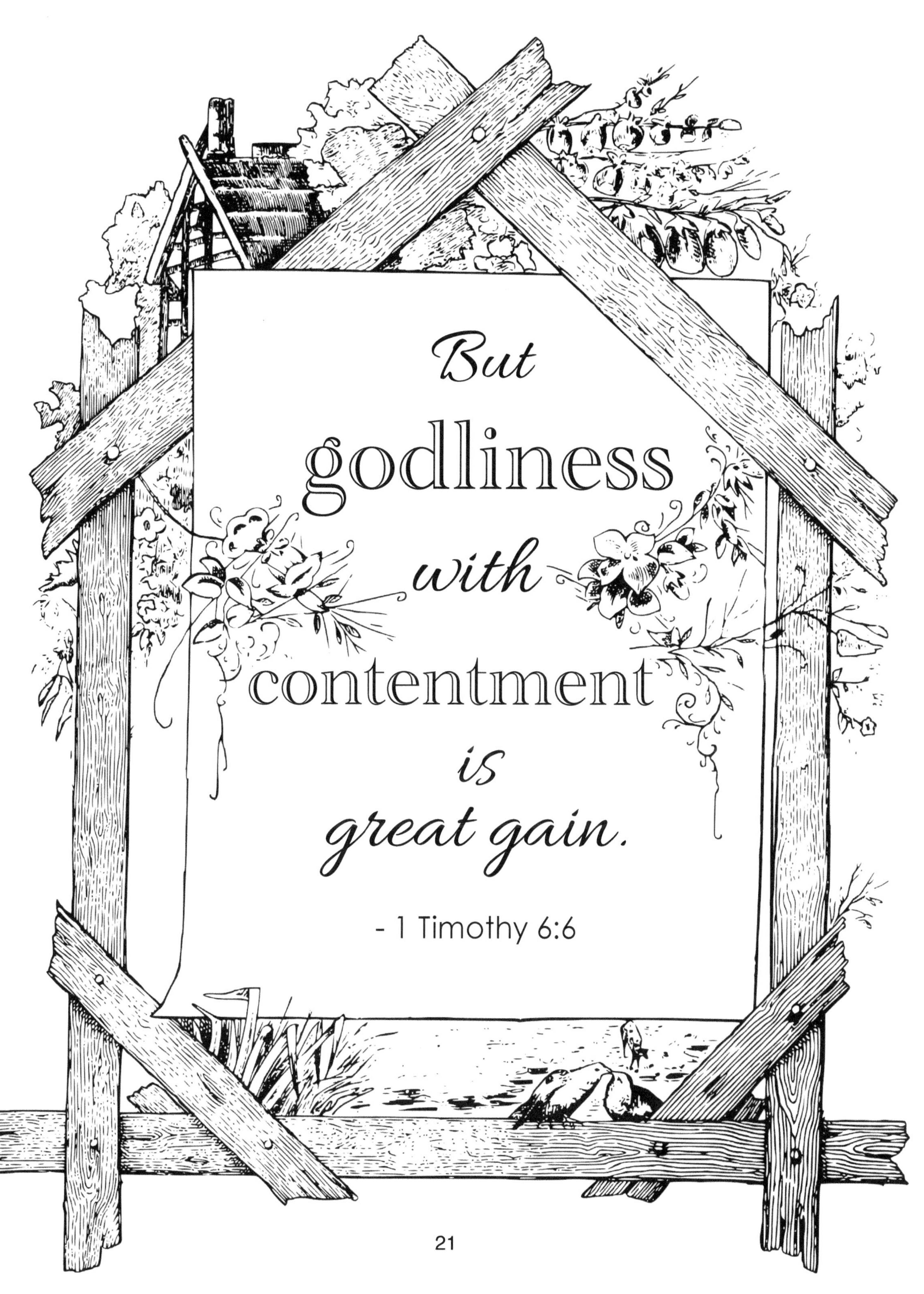
But
godliness
with
contentment
is
great gain.
- 1 Timothy 6:6

All Scripture is inspired
by God and profitable
for teaching, for reproof,
for correction, and
for training in righteousness.

–2 Timothy 3:16

Put on the Full Armor of God.

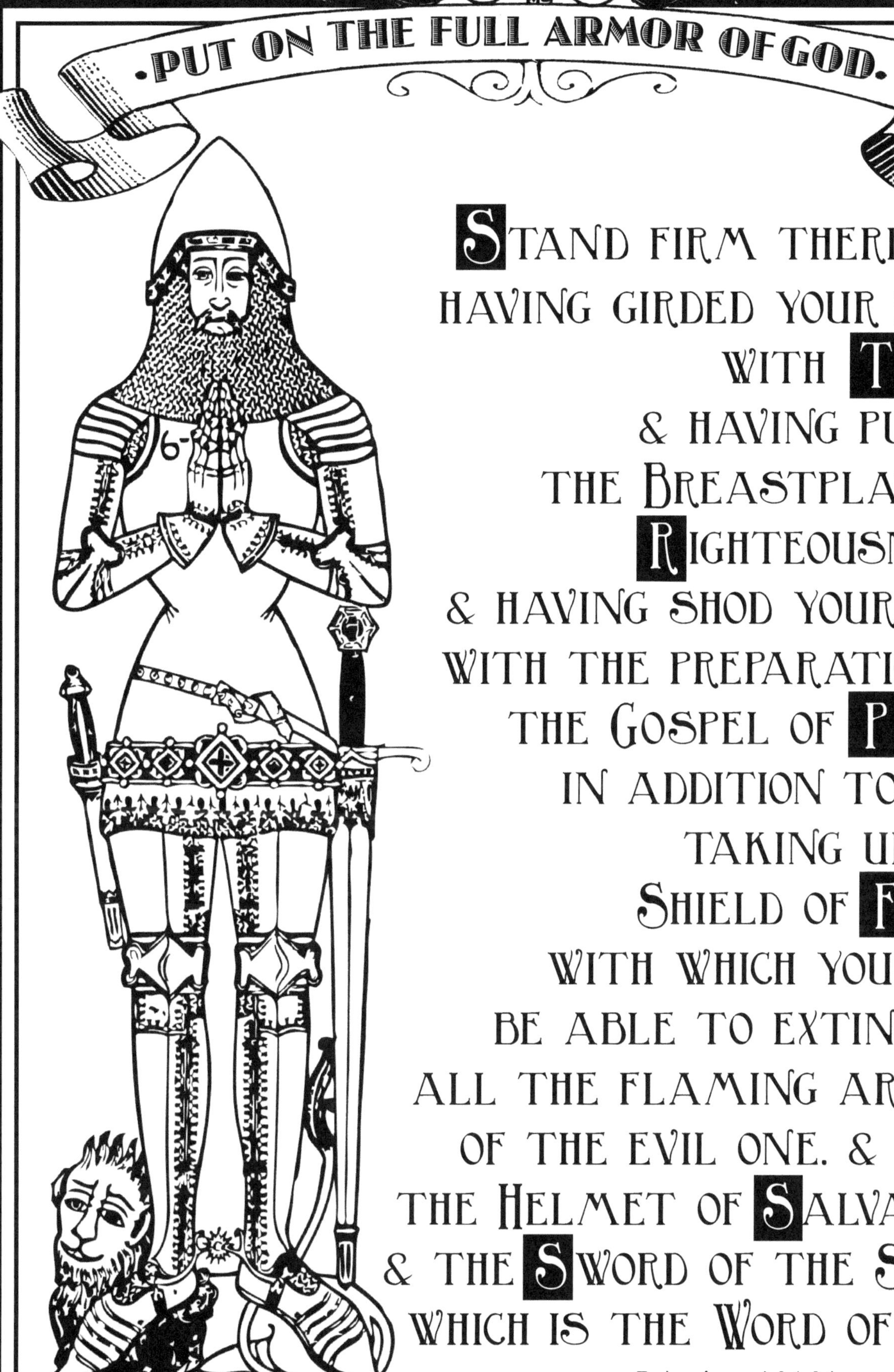

Stand firm therefore,
having girded your loins
with Truth,
& having put on
the Breastplate of
Righteousness,
& having shod your feet
with the preparation of
the Gospel of Peace;
in addition to all,
taking up the
Shield of Faith
with which you will
be able to extinguish
all the flaming arrows
of the evil one. & take
the Helmet of Salvation,
& the Sword of the Spirit,
which is the Word of God.

- Ephesians 6:14-16

All Scripture is inspired
by God and profitable
for teaching, for reproof,
for correction, and
for training in righteousness.

- 2 Timothy 3:16

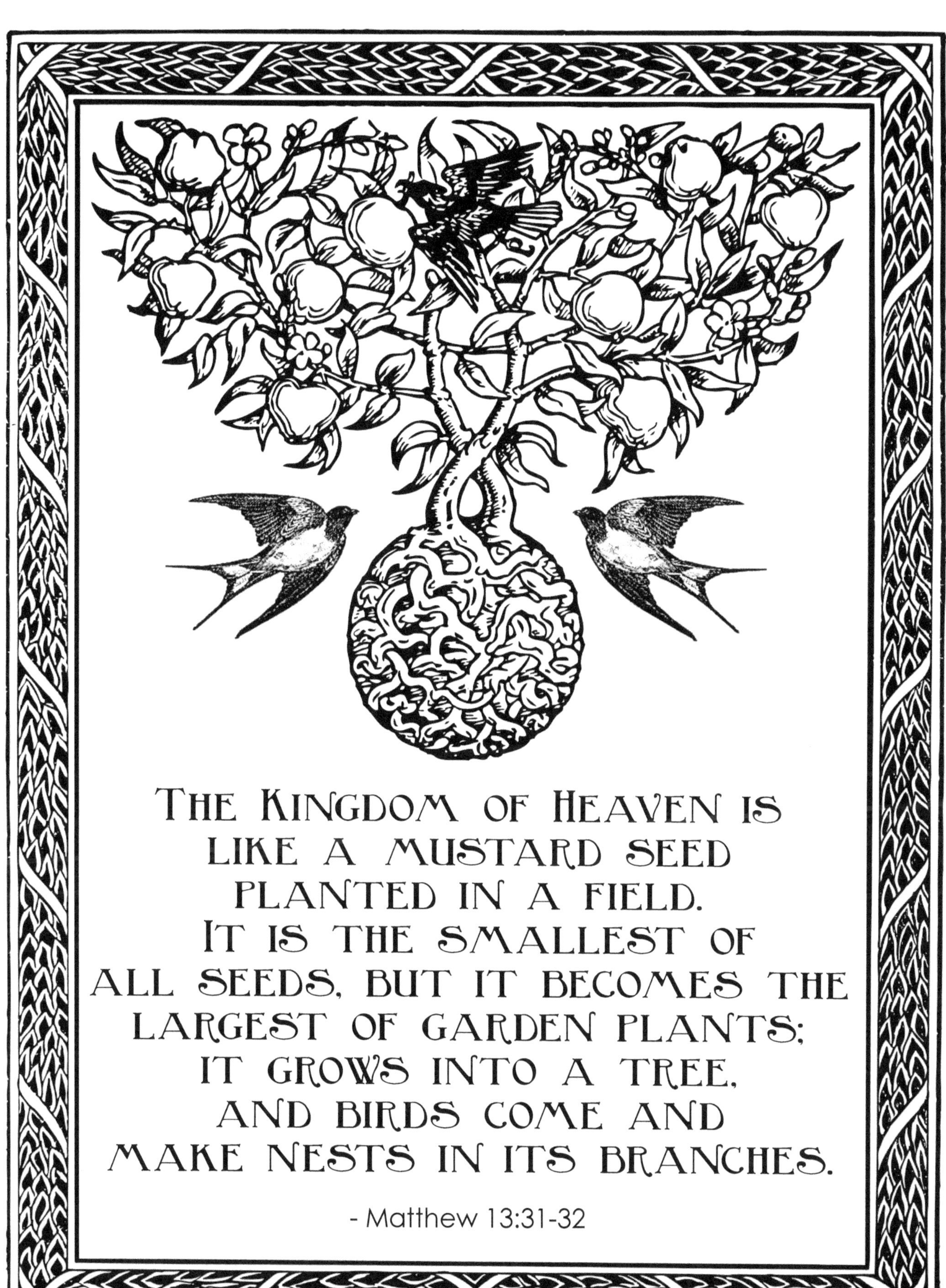

The Kingdom of Heaven is
like a mustard seed
planted in a field.
It is the smallest of
all seeds, but it becomes the
largest of garden plants;
it grows into a tree,
and birds come and
make nests in its branches.

- Matthew 13:31-32

All Scripture is inspired
by God and profitable
for teaching, for reproof,
for correction, and
for training in righteousness.

- 2 Timothy 3:16

"When
He
gives a
command,
even
the wind
and
waves
obey
Him!"

- Luke 8:25

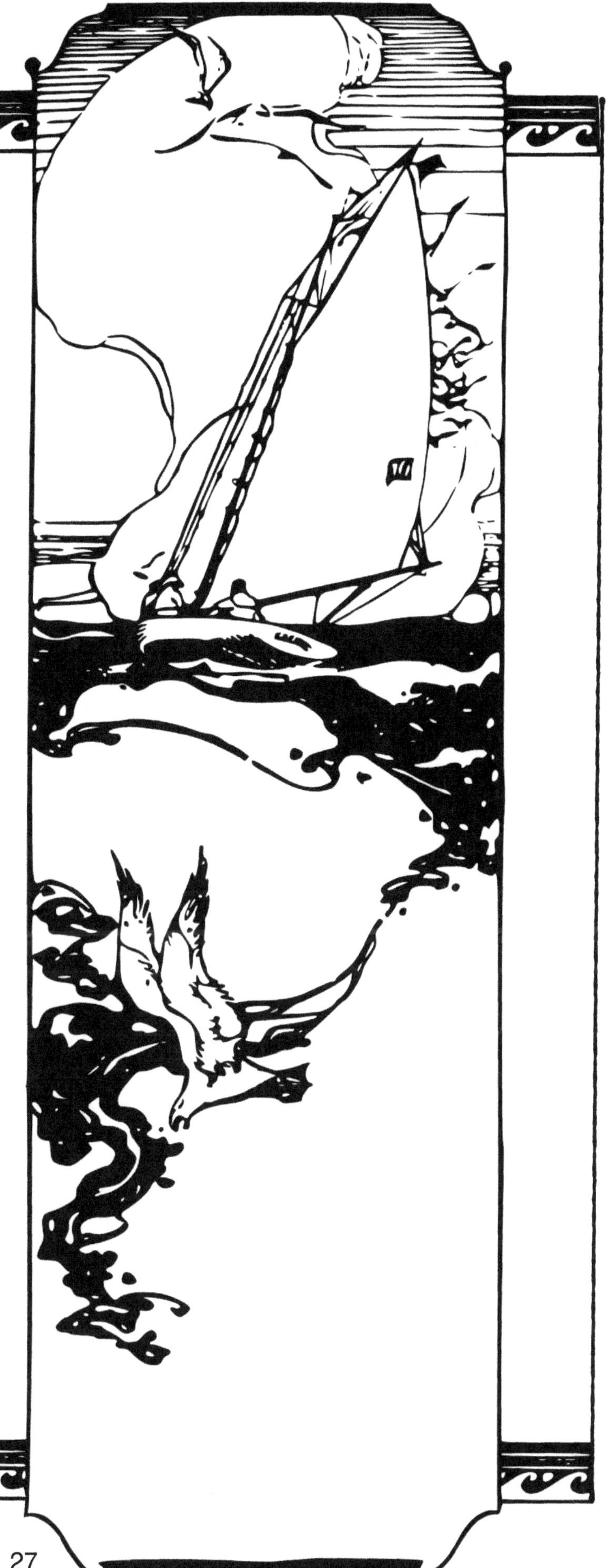

All Scripture is inspired
by God and profitable
for teaching, for reproof,
for correction, and
for training in righteousness.

- 2 Timothy 3:16

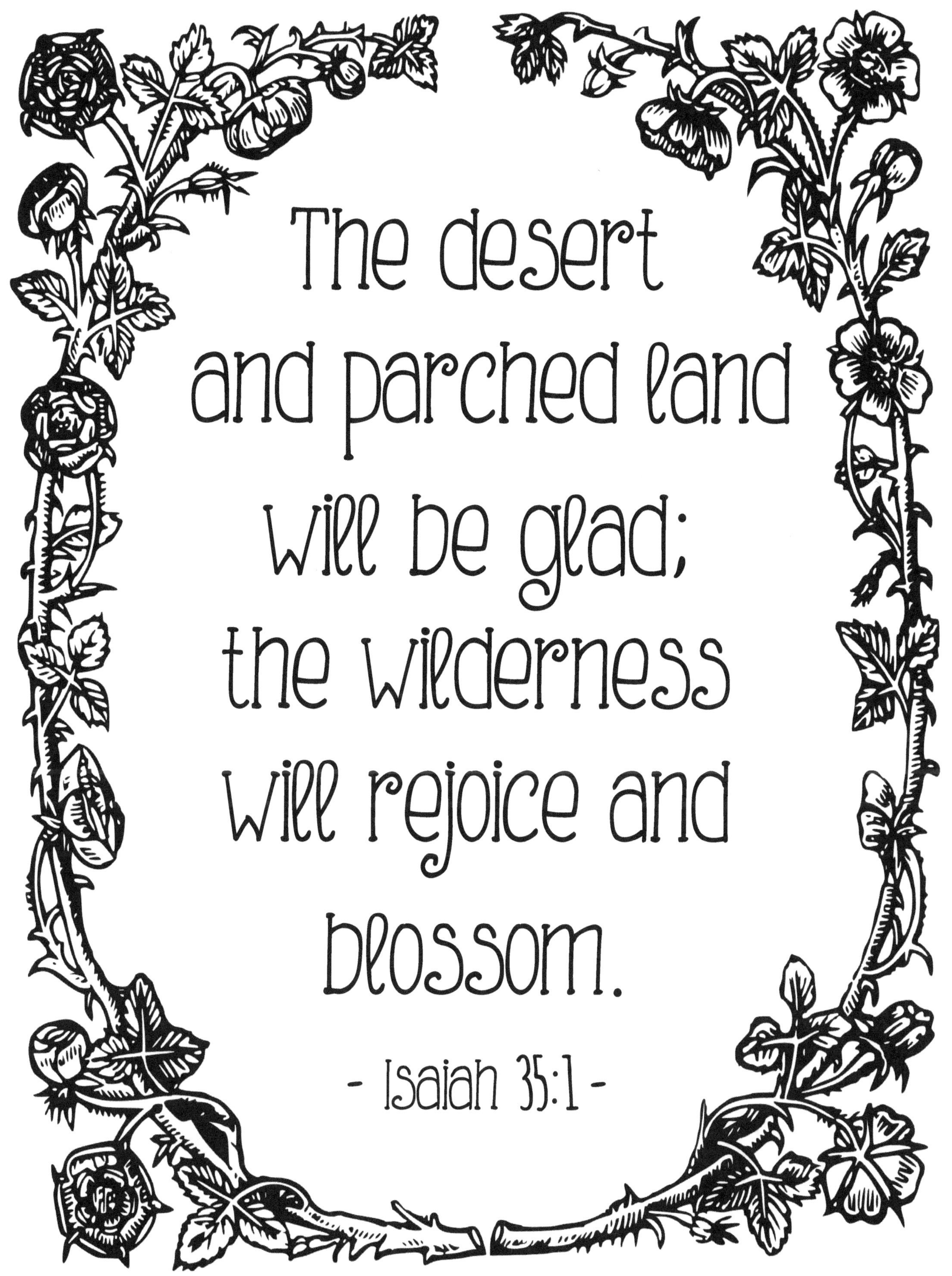
The desert
and parched land
will be glad;
the wilderness
will rejoice and
blossom.
- Isaiah 35:1 -

All Scripture is inspired
by God and profitable
for teaching, for reproof,
for correction, and
for training in righteousness.

- 2 Timothy 3:16

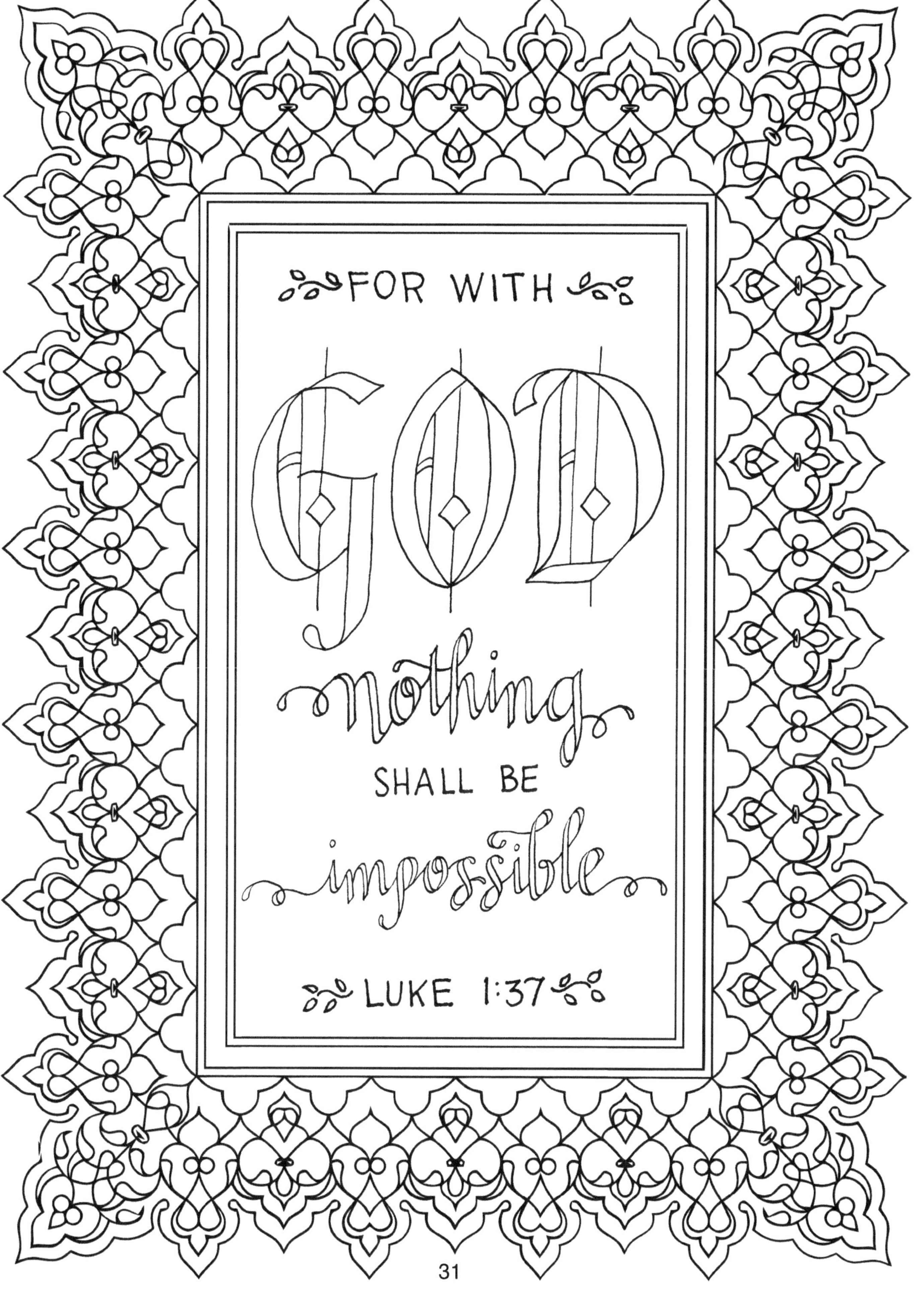
FOR WITH
GOD
nothing
SHALL BE
impossible
LUKE 1:37

All Scripture is inspired
by God and profitable
for teaching, for reproof,
for correction, and
for training in righteousness.

- 2 Timothy 3:16

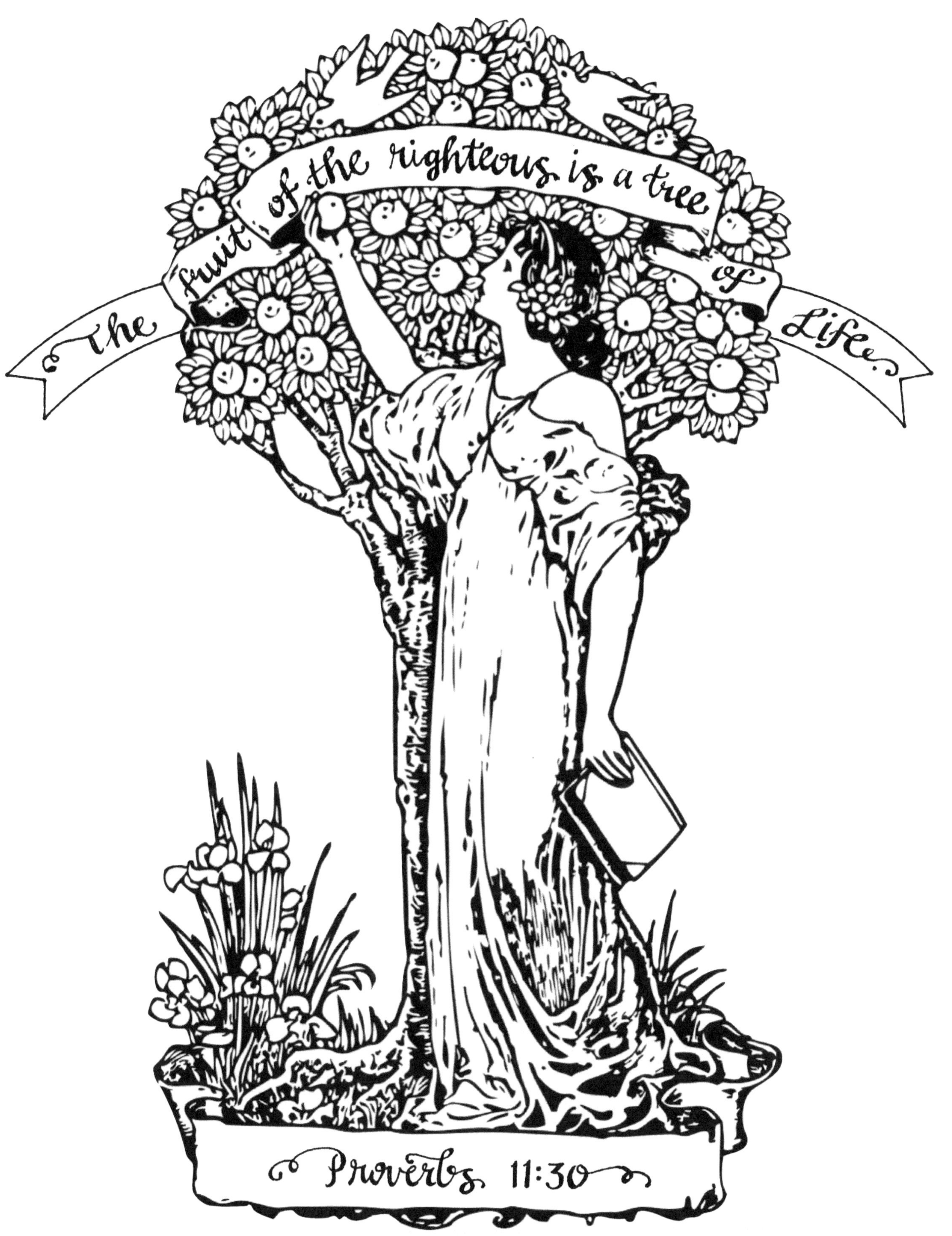
The fruit of the righteous is a tree of Life.
Proverbs 11:30

All Scripture is inspired
by God and profitable
for teaching, for reproof,
for correction, and
for training in righteousness.

- 2 Timothy 3:16

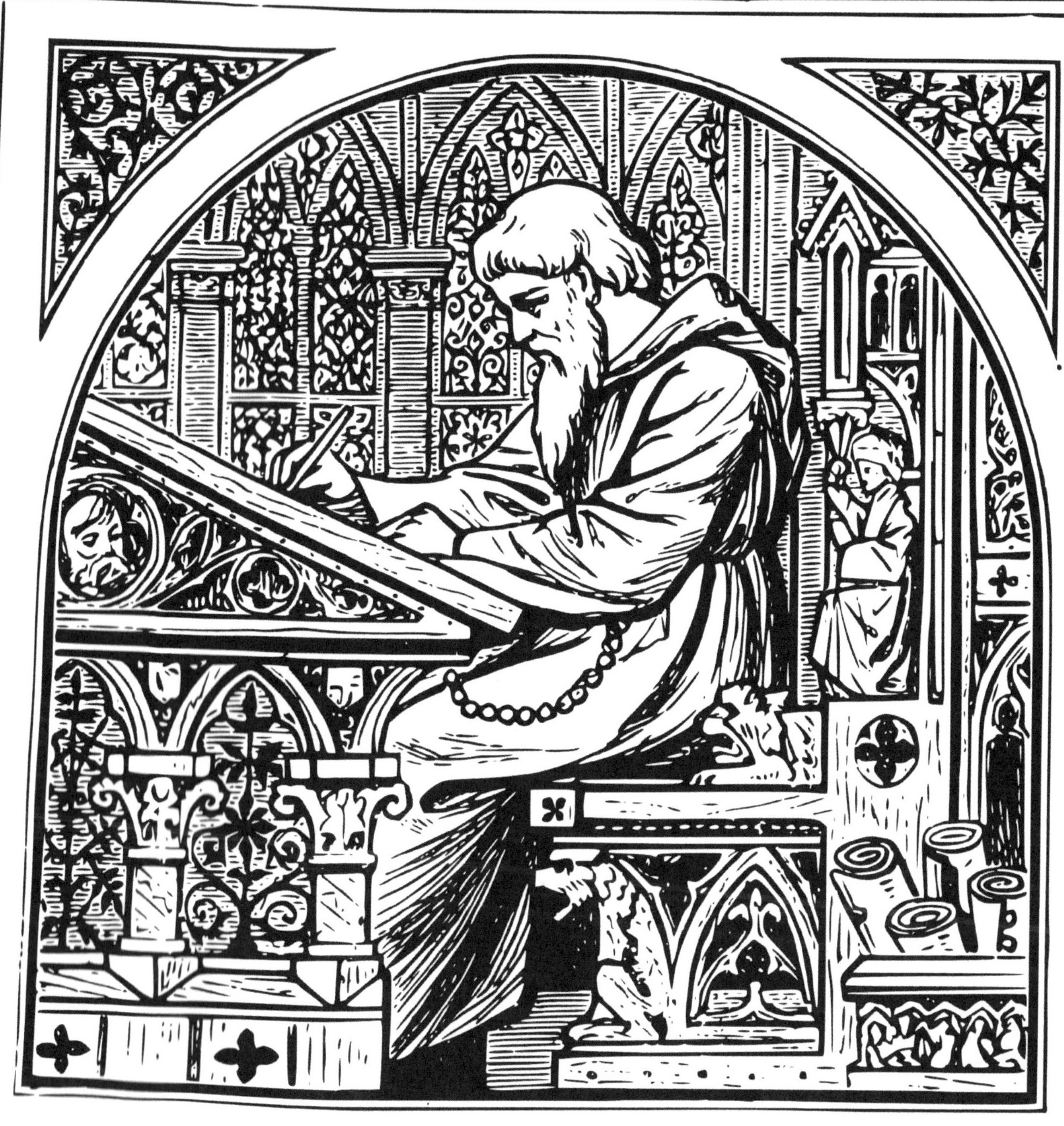

For no prophecy was ever made by an act of human will, but men moved by the Holy Spirit spoke from God.

- 2 Peter 1:21 -

All Scripture is inspired
by God and profitable
for teaching, for reproof,
for correction, and
for training in righteousness.

- 2 Timothy 3:16

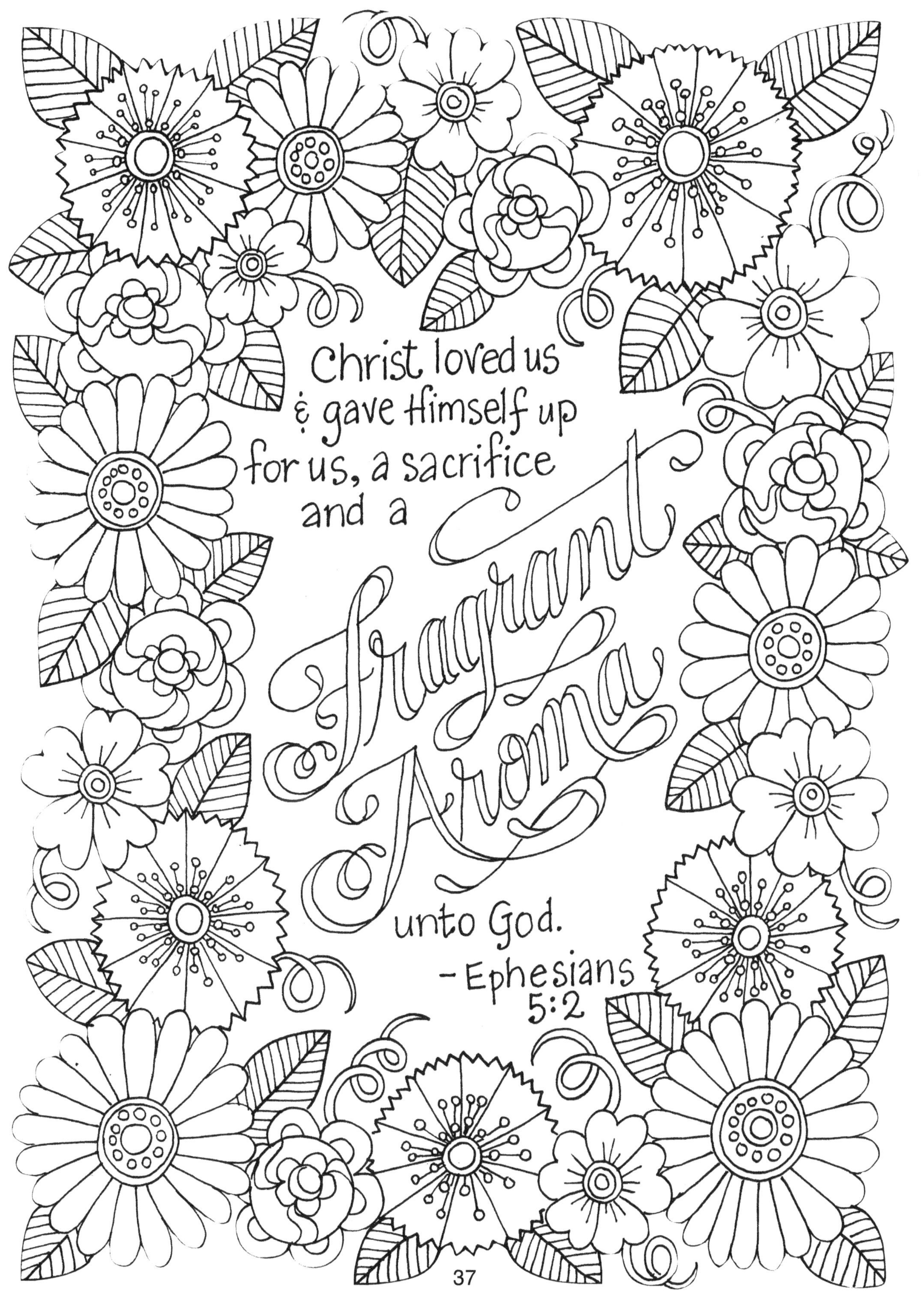
Christ loved us
& gave Himself up
for us, a sacrifice
and a
Fragrant
Aroma
unto God.
-Ephesians
5:2

All Scripture is inspired
by God and profitable
for teaching, for reproof,
for correction, and
for training in righteousness.

- 2 Timothy 3:16

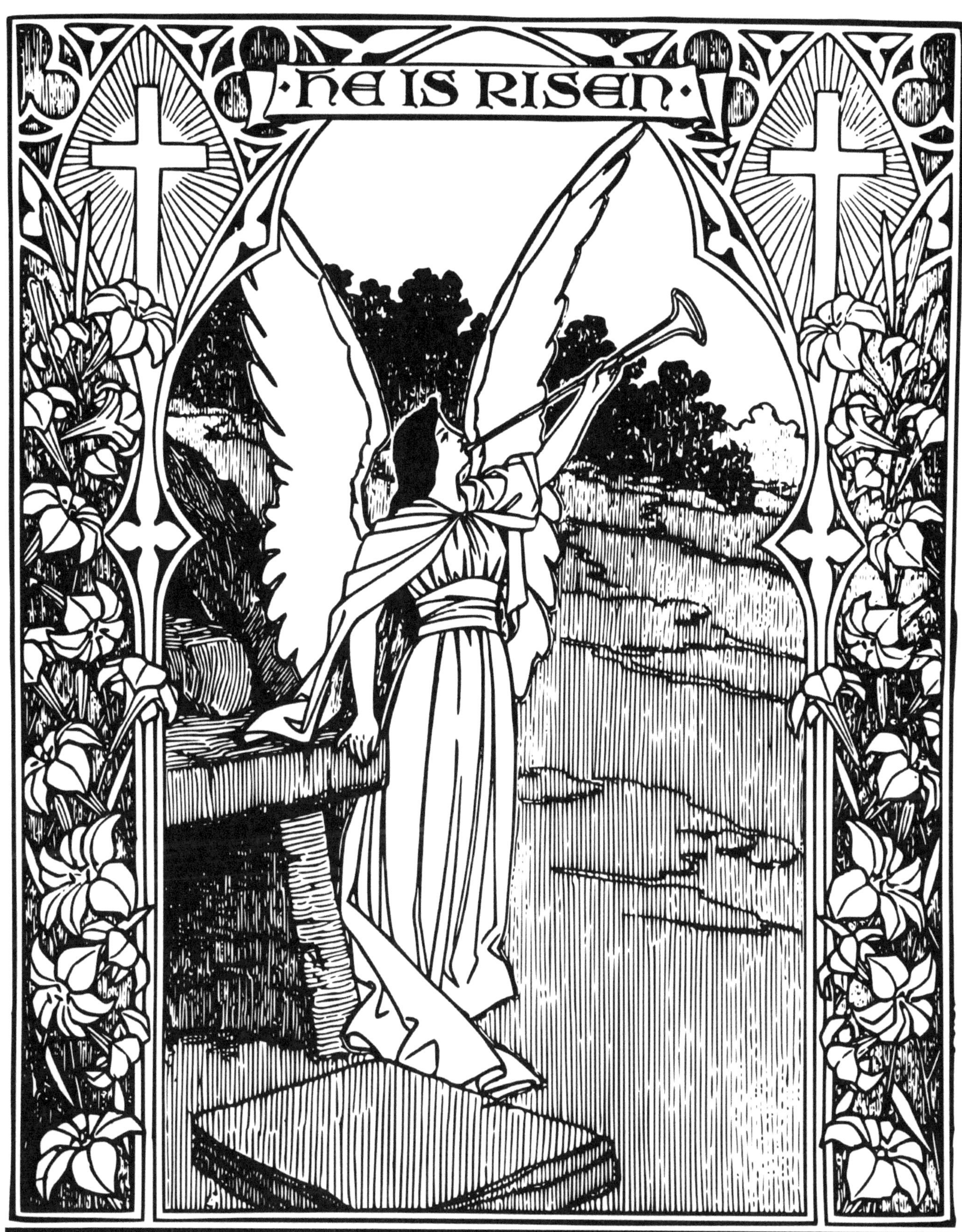

Matthew 28:6

All Scripture is inspired
by God and profitable
for teaching, for reproof,
for correction, and
for training in righteousness.

- 2 Timothy 3:16

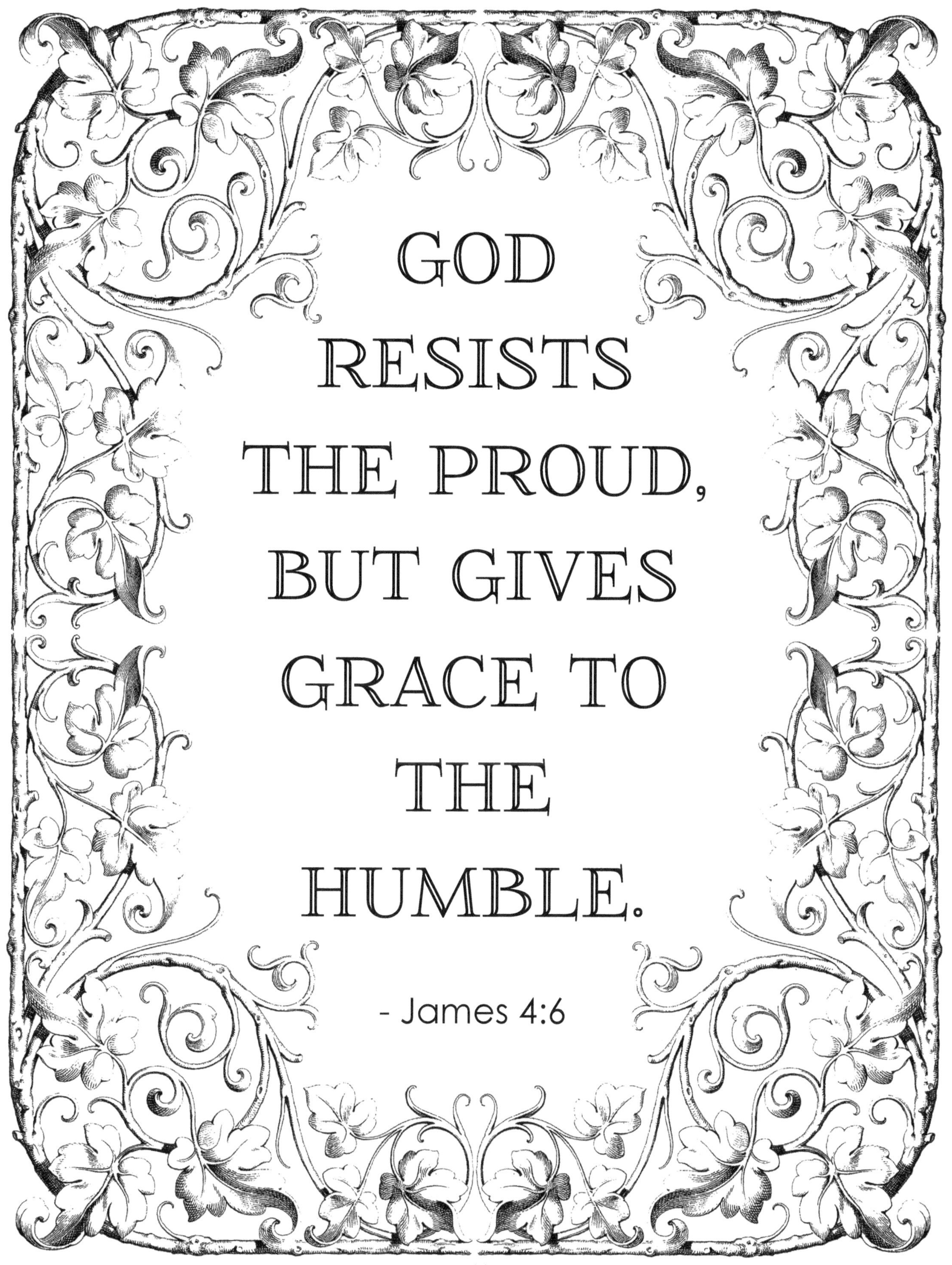

GOD RESISTS THE PROUD, BUT GIVES GRACE TO THE HUMBLE.

- James 4:6

All Scripture is inspired
by God and profitable
for teaching, for reproof,
for correction, and
for training in righteousness.

- 2 Timothy 3:16

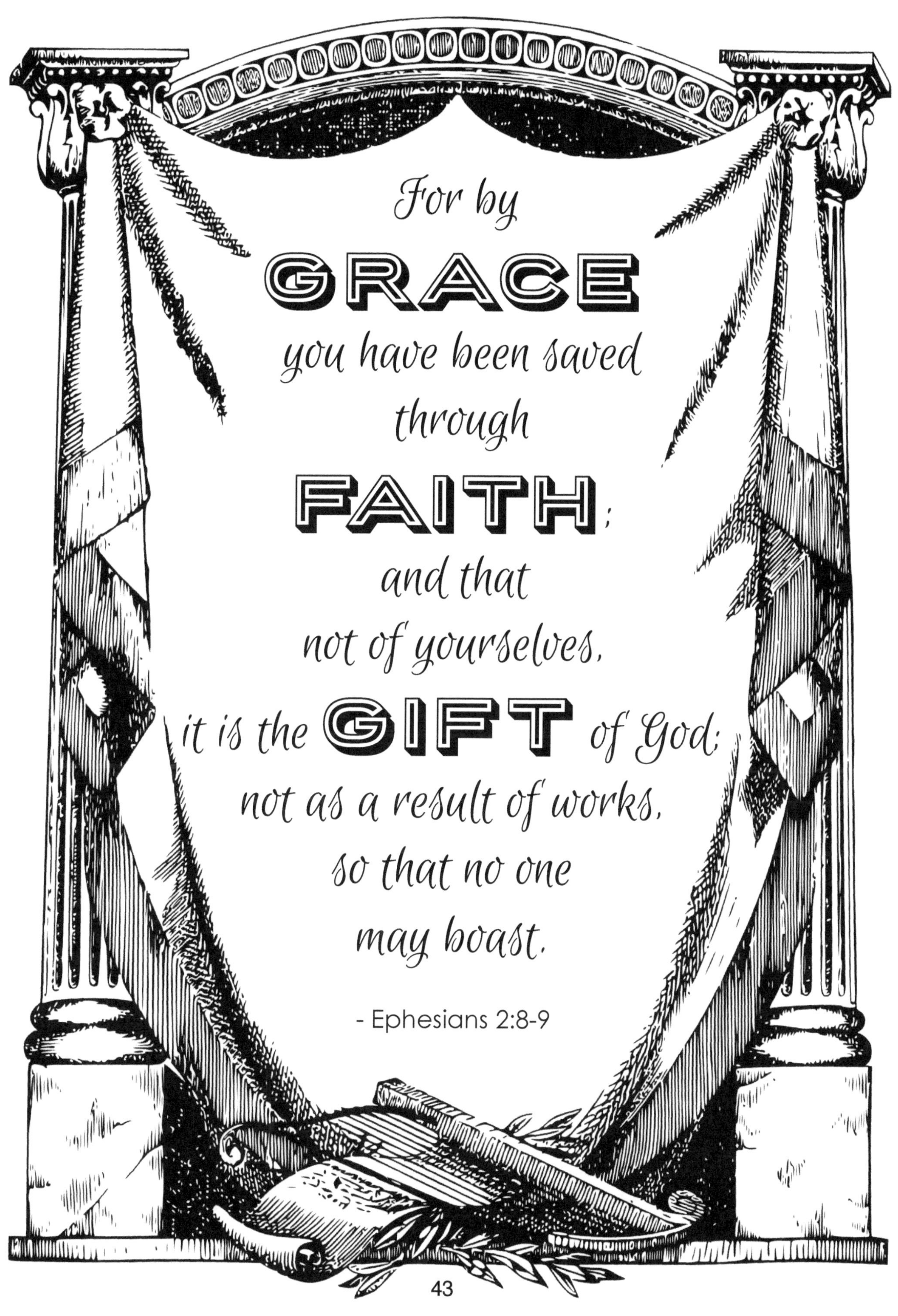
For by
GRACE
you have been saved
through
FAITH;
and that
not of yourselves,
it is the GIFT of God;
not as a result of works,
so that no one
may boast.
- Ephesians 2:8-9

All Scripture is inspired
by God and profitable
for teaching, for reproof,
for correction, and
for training in righteousness.

- 2 Timothy 3:16

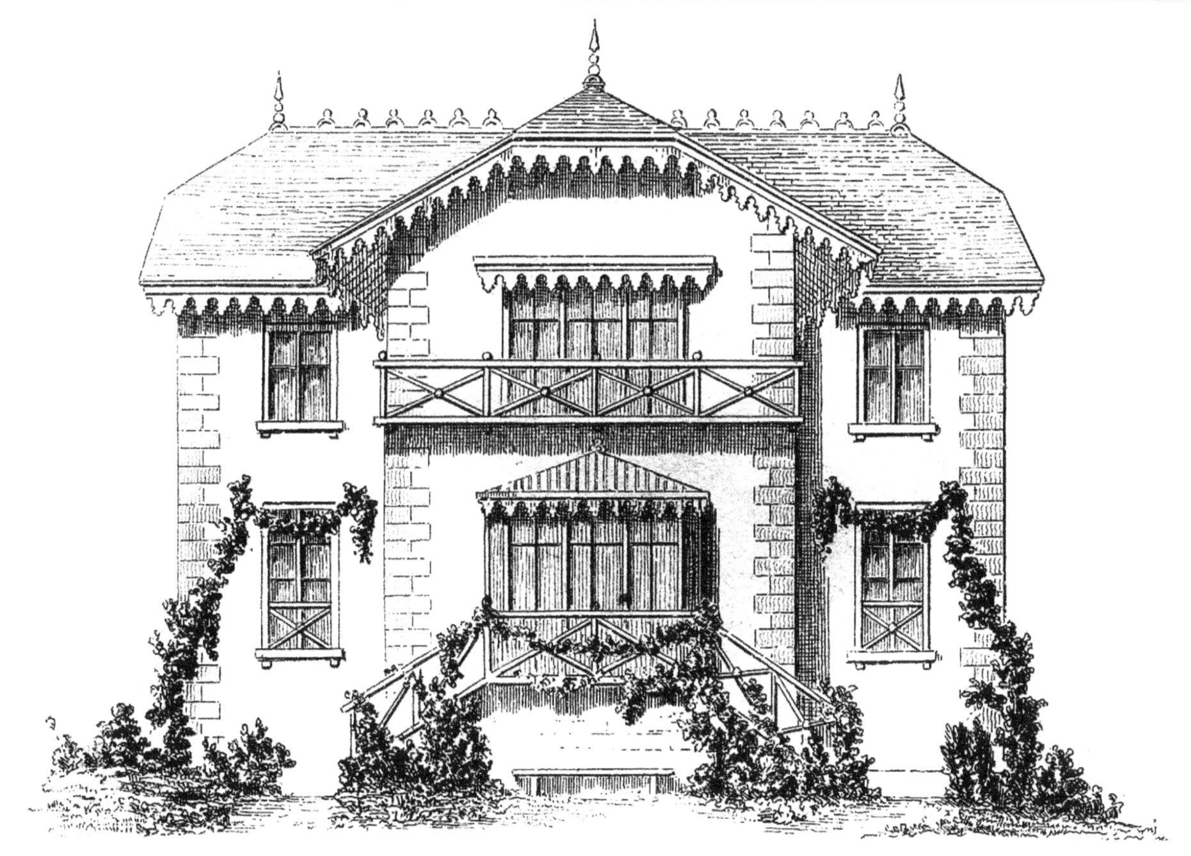

BY **WISDOM** A HOUSE IS BUILT, BY

UNDERSTANDING

IT IS ESTABLISHED,

AND BY **KNOWLEDGE**

THE ROOMS ARE FILLED WITH ALL PRECIOUS AND PLEASANT RICHES.

All Scripture is inspired
by God and profitable
for teaching, for reproof,
for correction, and
for training in righteousness.

- 2 Timothy 3:16

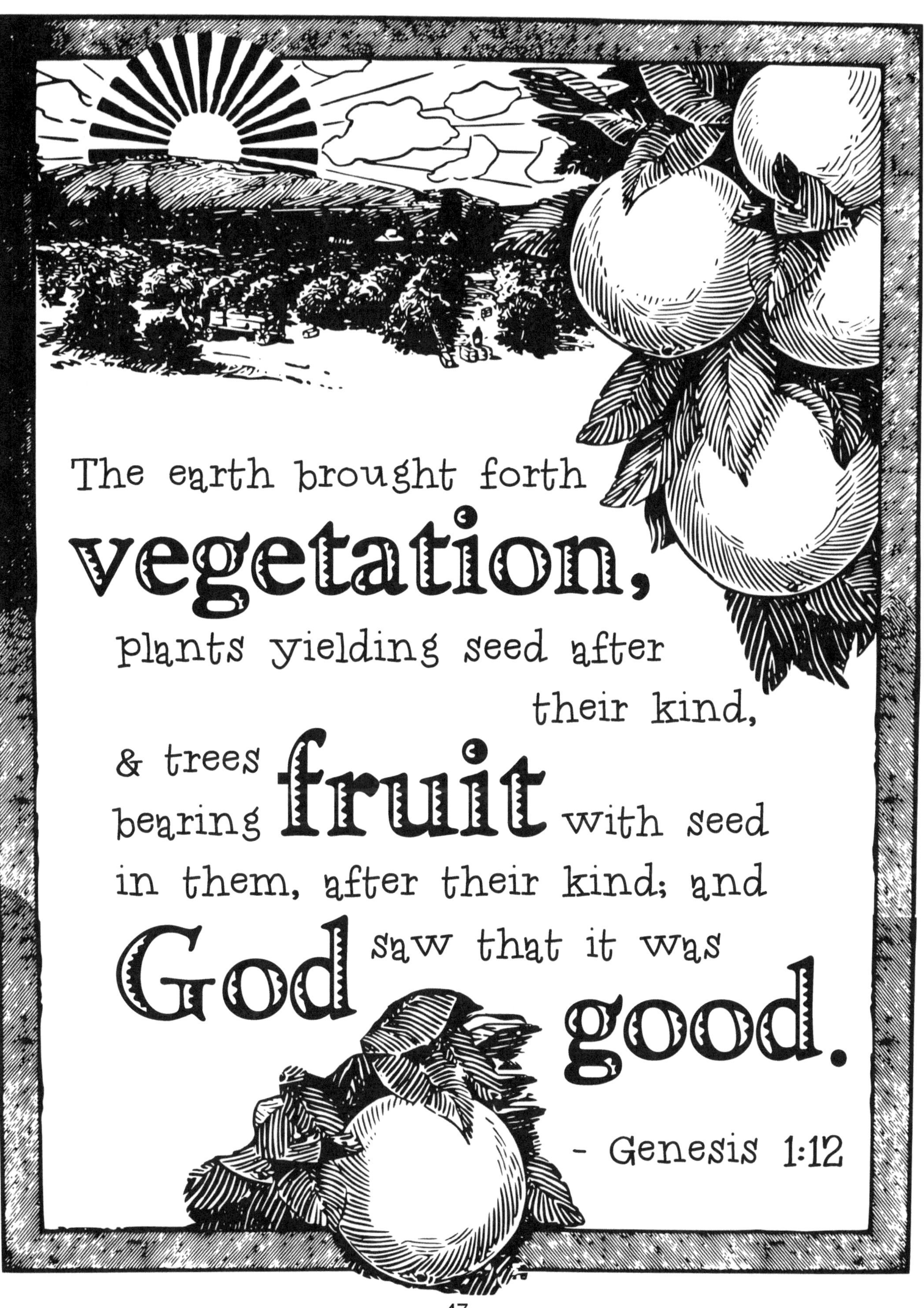
The earth brought forth
vegetation,
plants yielding seed after
their kind,
& trees
bearing fruit with seed
in them, after their kind; and
God saw that it was
good.
- Genesis 1:12

All Scripture is inspired
by God and profitable
for teaching, for reproof,
for correction, and
for training in righteousness.

- 2 Timothy 3:16

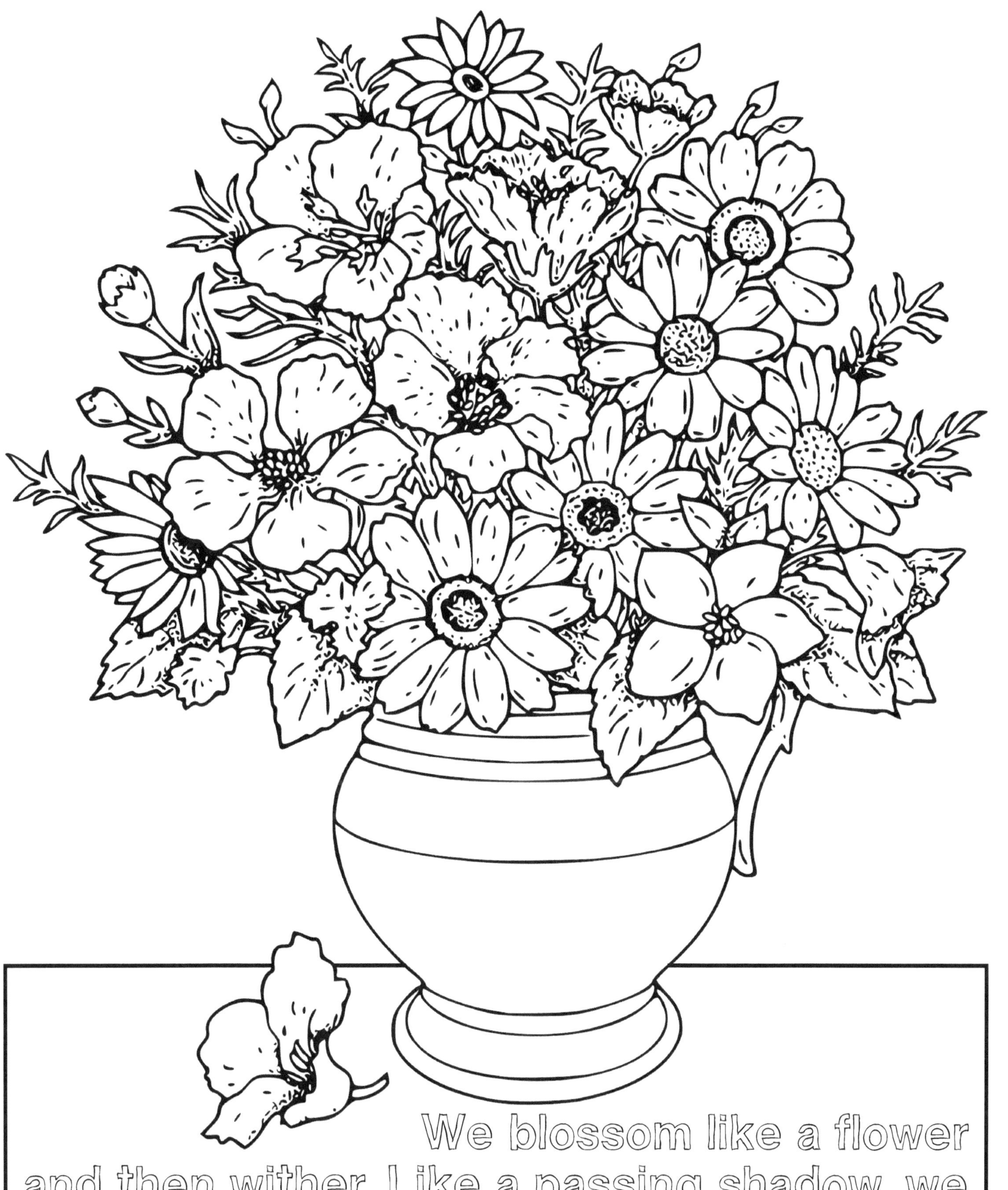

We blossom like a flower and then wither. Like a passing shadow, we quickly disappear.

– Job 14:2, NLT

All Scripture is inspired
by God and profitable
for teaching, for reproof,
for correction, and
for training in righteousness.

- 2 Timothy 3:16

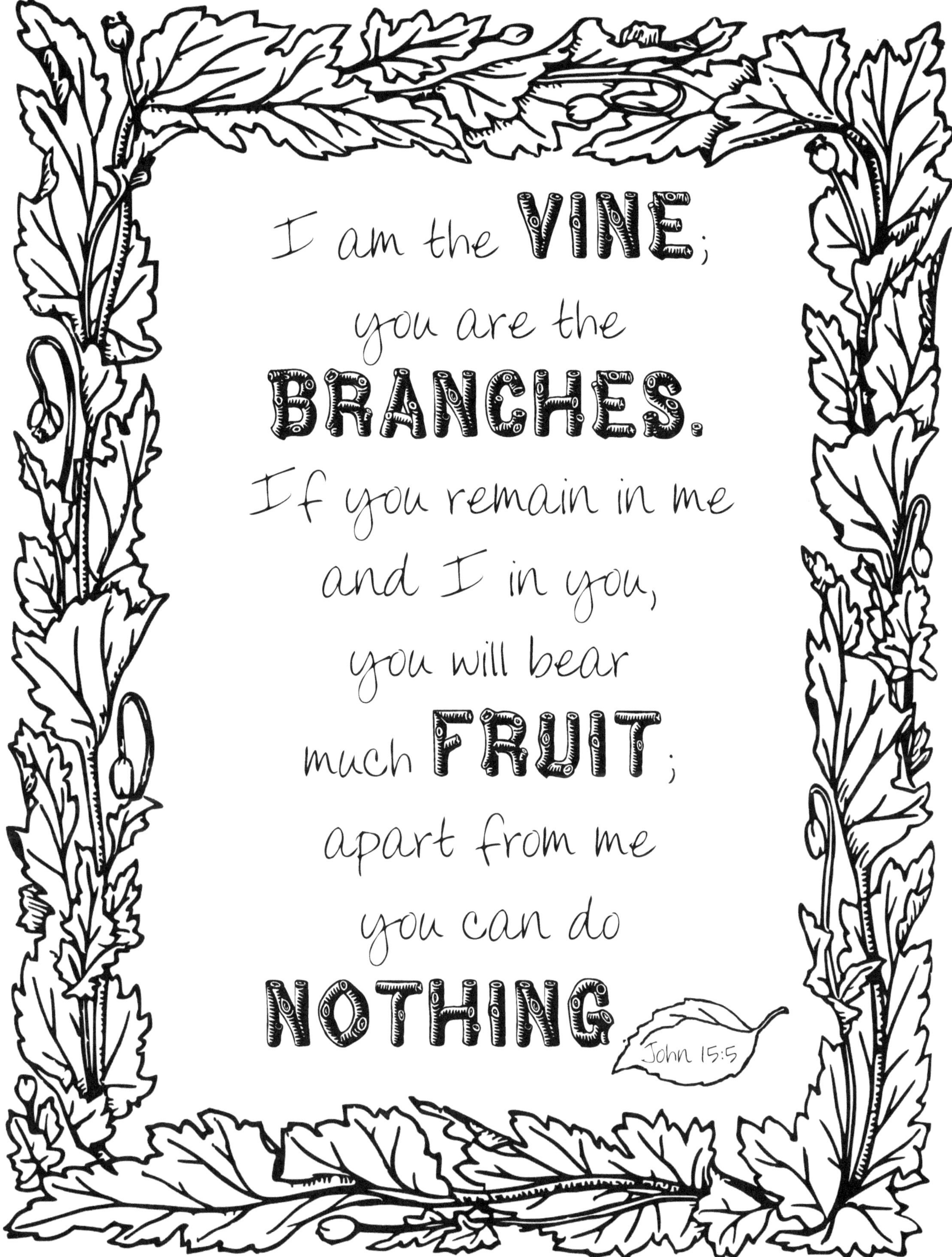
I am the VINE;
you are the
BRANCHES.
If you remain in me
and I in you,
you will bear
much FRUIT;
apart from me
you can do
NOTHING.
John 15:5

All Scripture is inspired
by God and profitable
for teaching, for reproof,
for correction, and
for training in righteousness.

- 2 Timothy 3:16

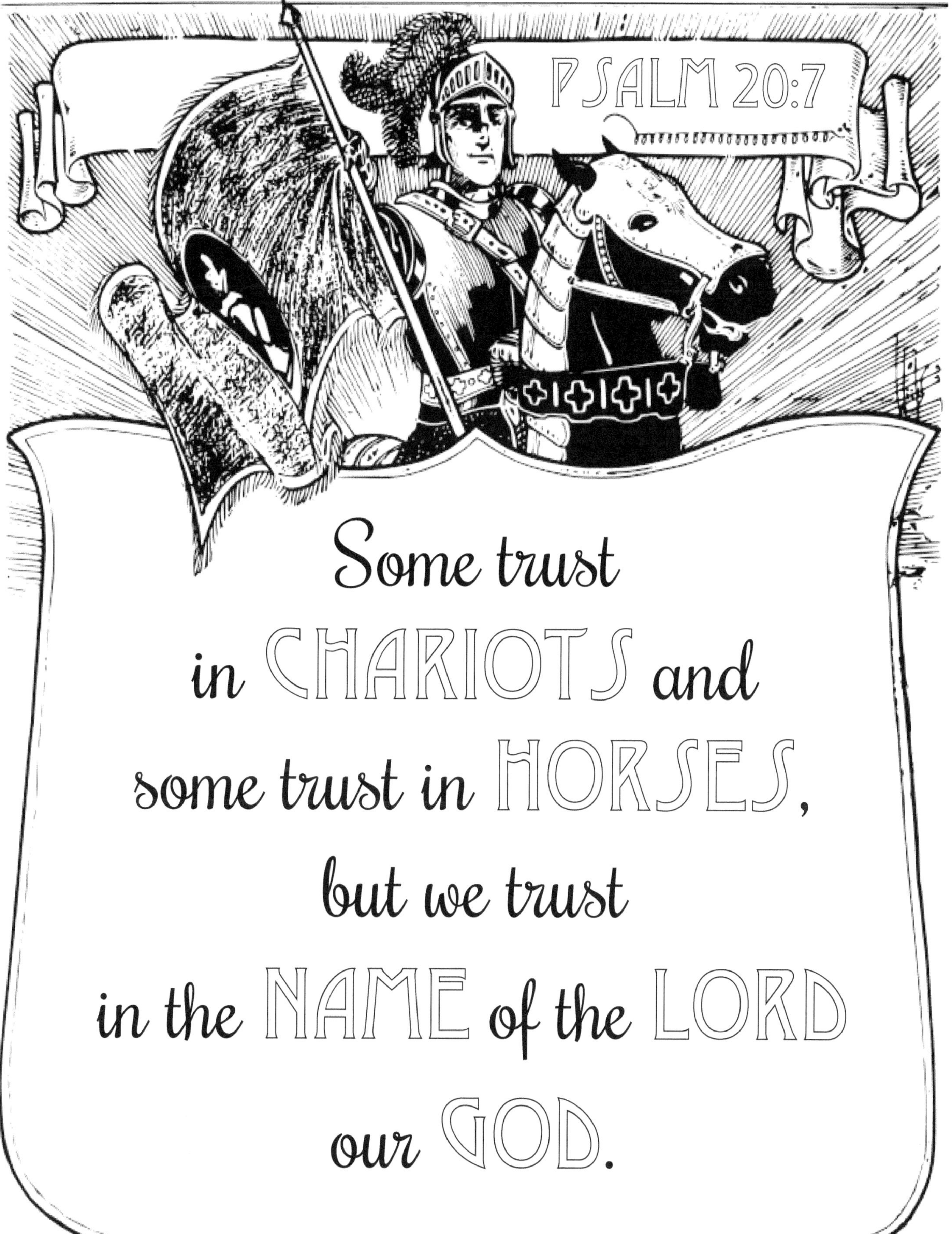
PSALM 20:7
Some trust
in CHARIOTS and
some trust in HORSES,
but we trust
in the NAME of the LORD
our GOD.

All Scripture is inspired
by God and profitable
for teaching, for reproof,
for correction, and
for training in righteousness.

- 2 Timothy 3:16

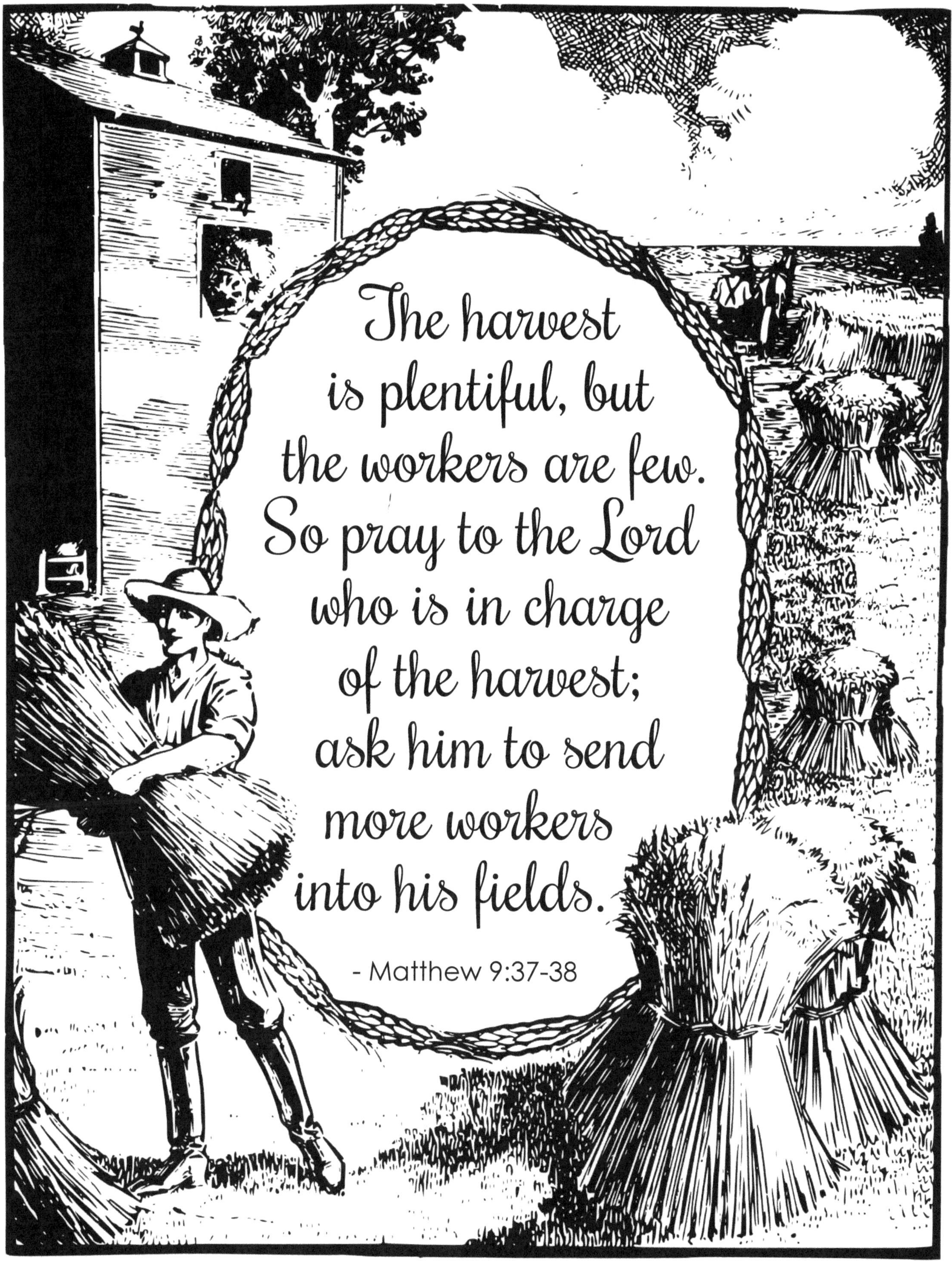
The harvest
is plentiful, but
the workers are few.
So pray to the Lord
who is in charge
of the harvest;
ask him to send
more workers
into his fields.
- Matthew 9:37-38

All Scripture is inspired
by God and profitable
for teaching, for reproof,
for correction, and
for training in righteousness.

- 2 Timothy 3:16

PSALM 127:3-5♡

Children are a blessing from the LORD...
Happy is the man whose Quiver is full of them.

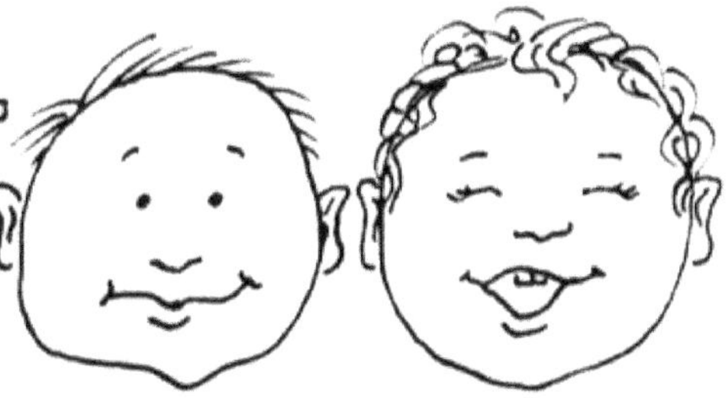

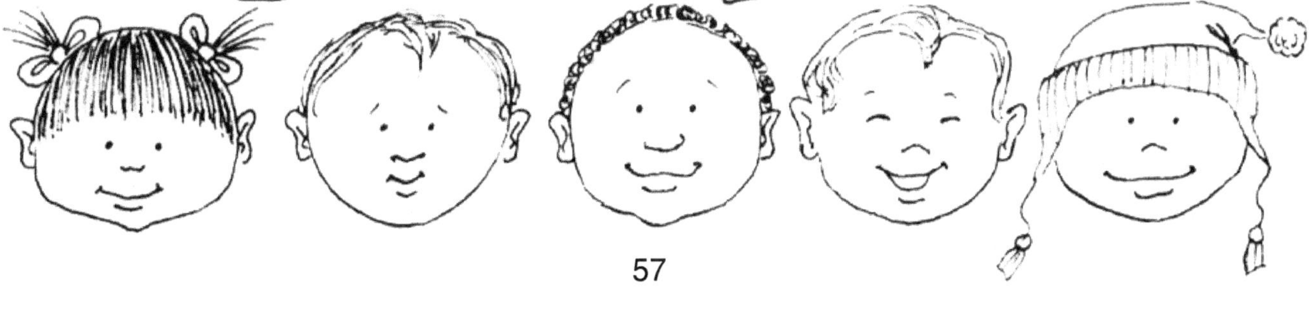

All Scripture is inspired
by God and profitable
for teaching, for reproof,
for correction, and
for training in righteousness.

- 2 Timothy 3:16

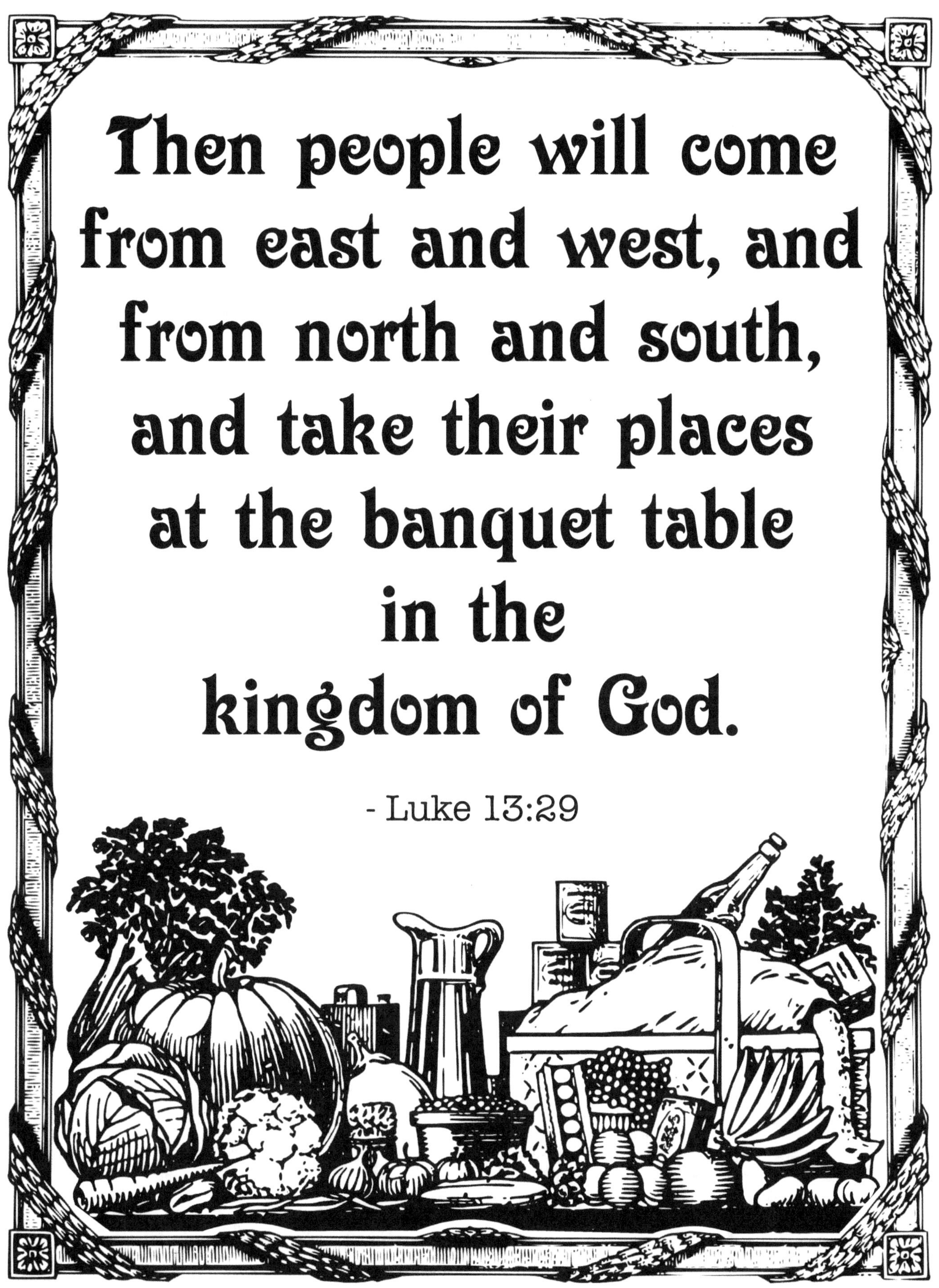

Then people will come from east and west, and from north and south, and take their places at the banquet table in the kingdom of God.

- Luke 13:29

All Scripture is inspired
by God and profitable
for teaching, for reproof,
for correction, and
for training in righteousness.

- 2 Timothy 3:16

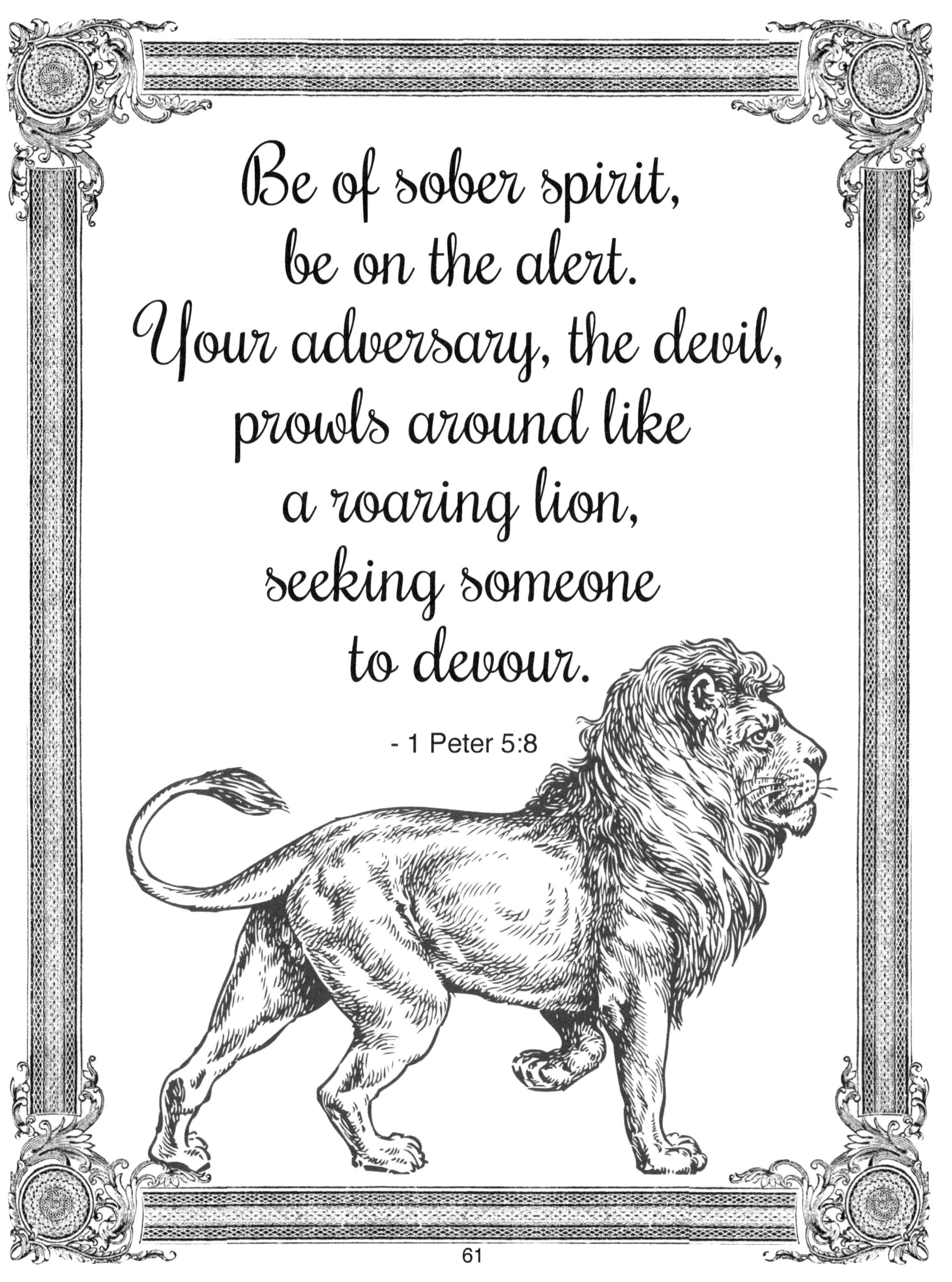

Be of sober spirit,
be on the alert.
Your adversary, the devil,
prowls around like
a roaring lion,
seeking someone
to devour.

- 1 Peter 5:8

All Scripture is inspired
by God and profitable
for teaching, for reproof,
for correction, and
for training in righteousness.

- 2 Timothy 3:16

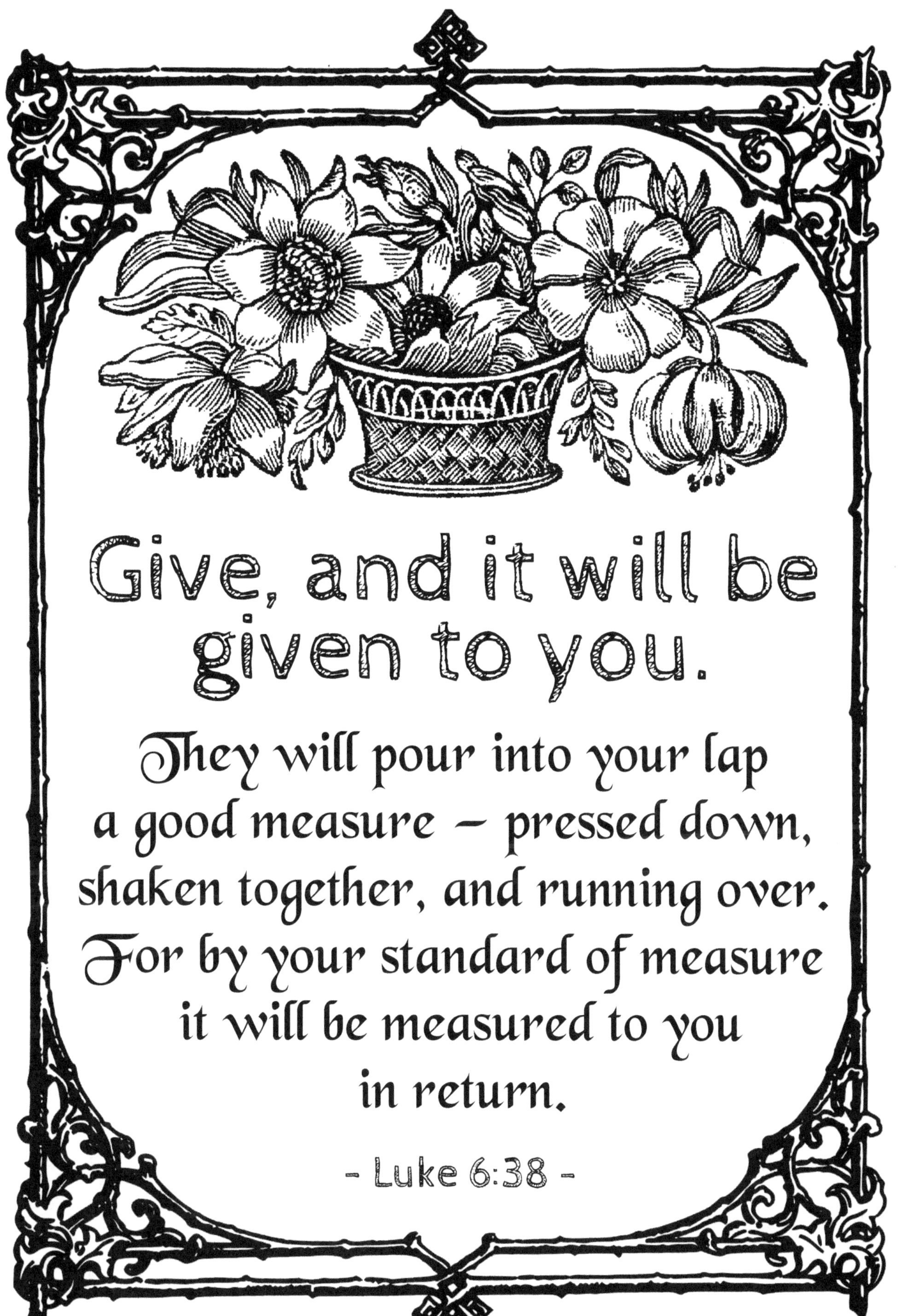
Give, and it will be given to you.
They will pour into your lap a good measure – pressed down, shaken together, and running over. For by your standard of measure it will be measured to you in return.
- Luke 6:38 -

All Scripture is inspired
by God and profitable
for teaching, for reproof,
for correction, and
for training in righteousness.

- 2 Timothy 3:16

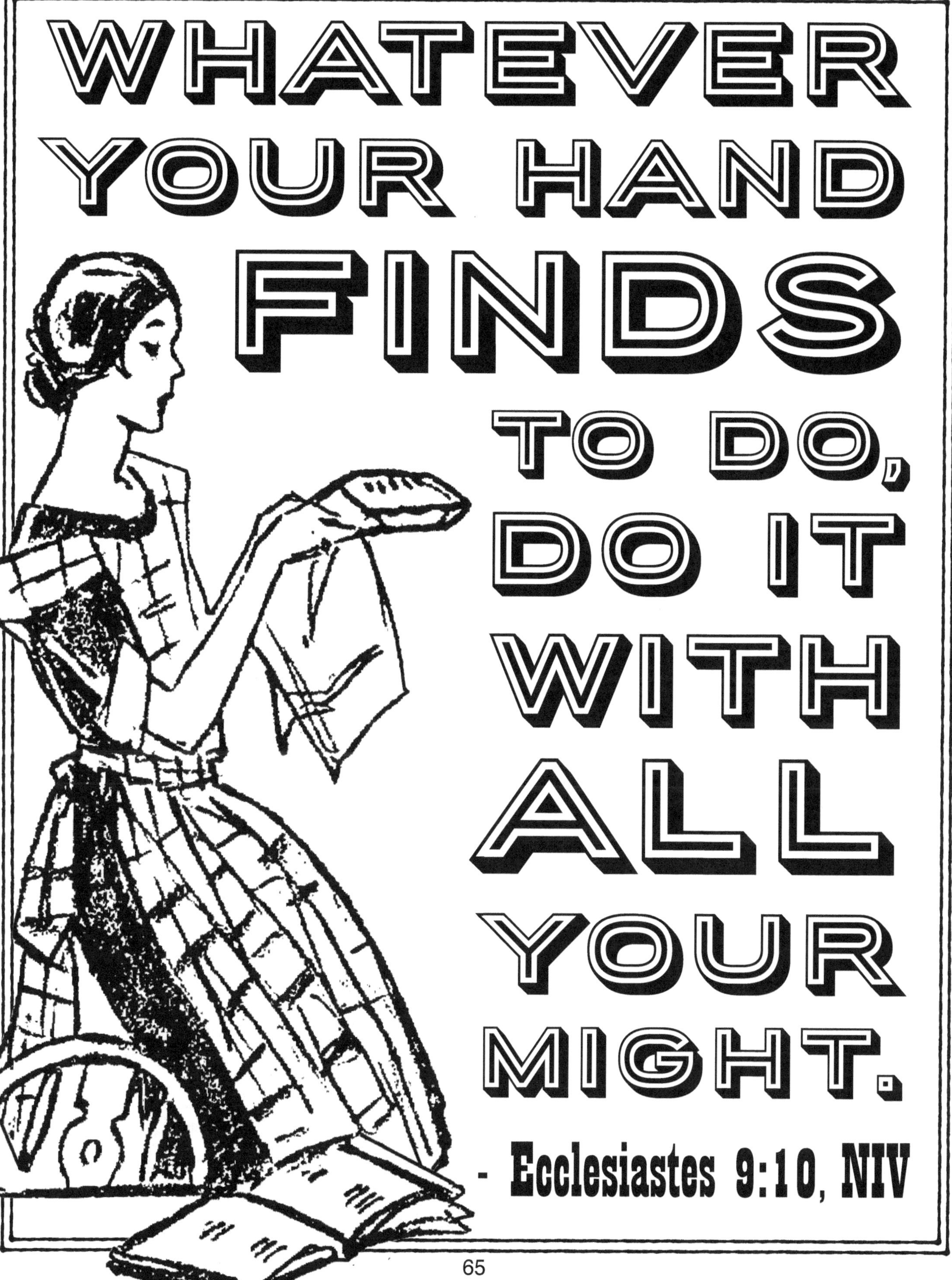
WHATEVER YOUR HAND FINDS TO DO, DO IT WITH ALL YOUR MIGHT.
- Ecclesiastes 9:10, NIV

All Scripture is inspired
by God and profitable
for teaching, for reproof,
for correction, and
for training in righteousness.

- 2 Timothy 3:16

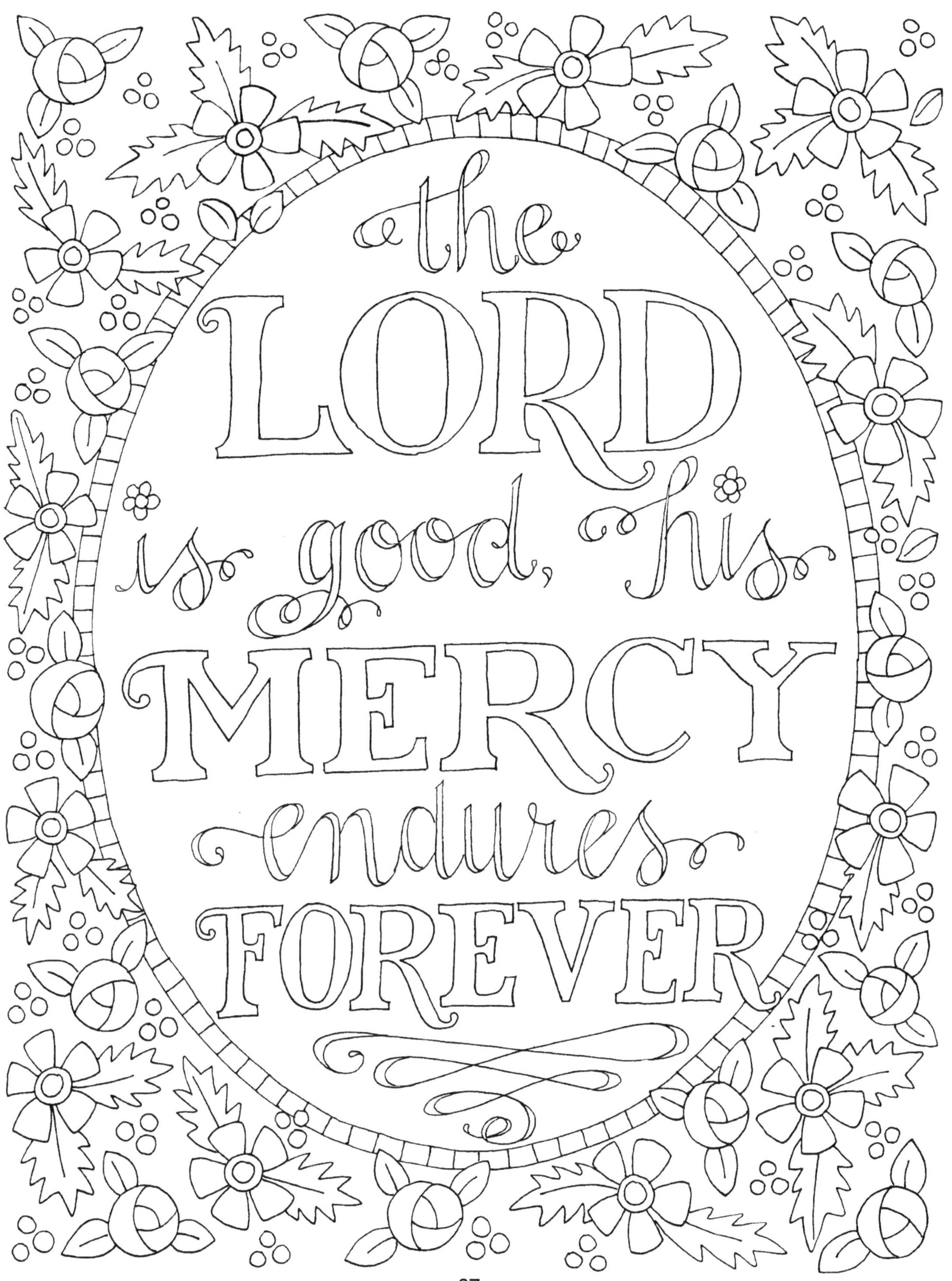
the
LORD
is good, his
MERCY
endures
FOREVER

All Scripture is inspired
by God and profitable
for teaching, for reproof,
for correction, and
for training in righteousness.

- 2 Timothy 3:16

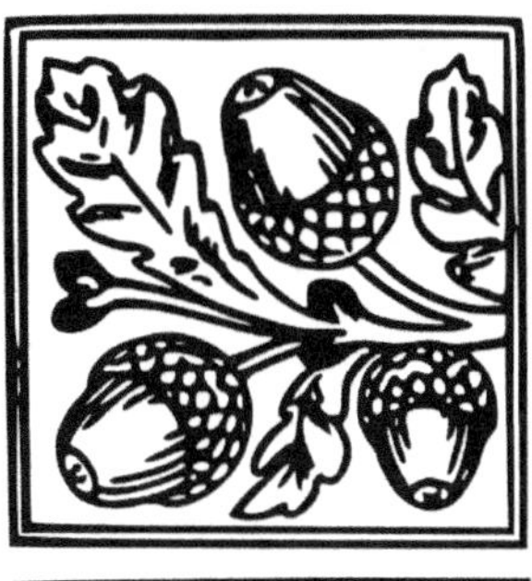

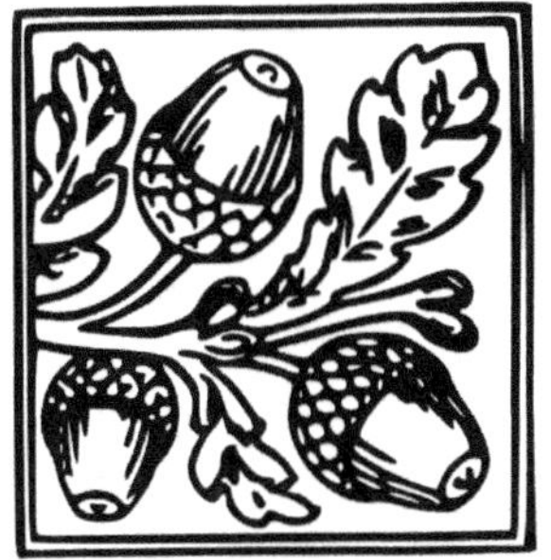
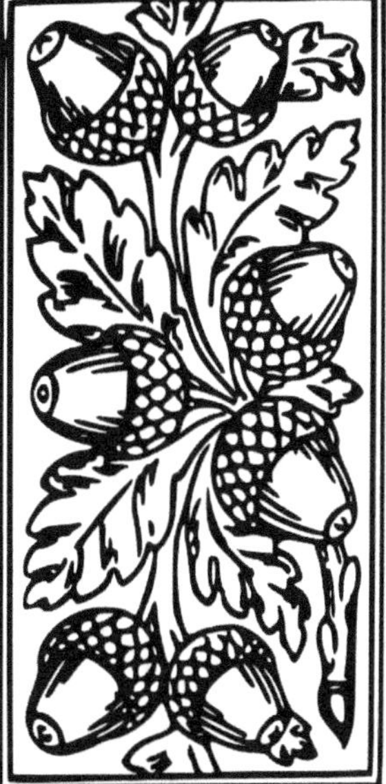

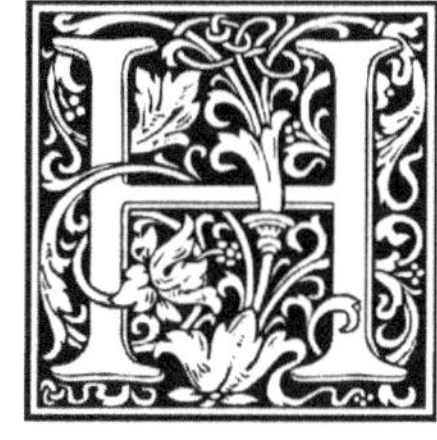

e cuts off every branch in me that bears no fruit, while

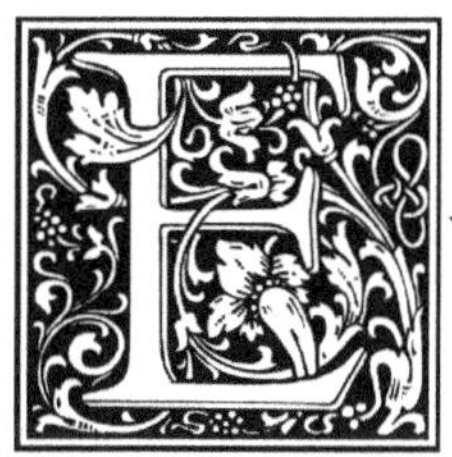

very branch that does bear fruit he prunes so that it will be even

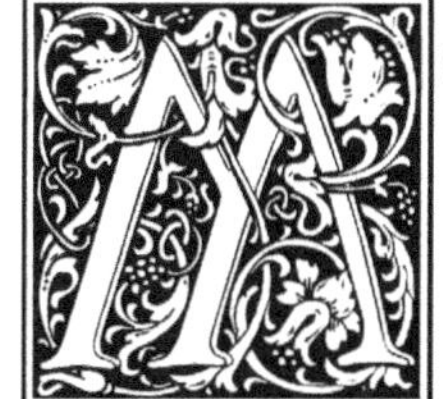

ore fruitful.

- John 15:2

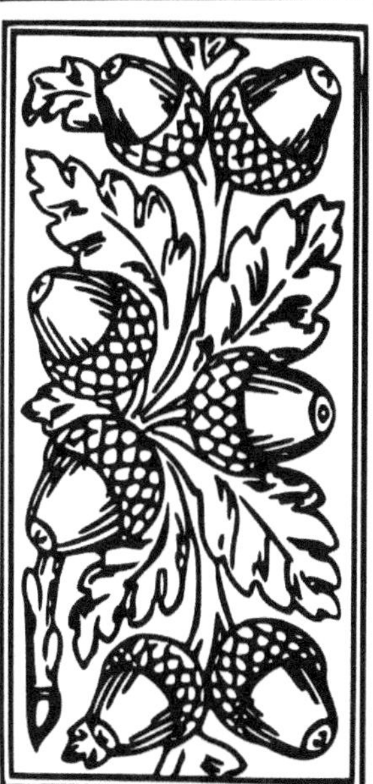
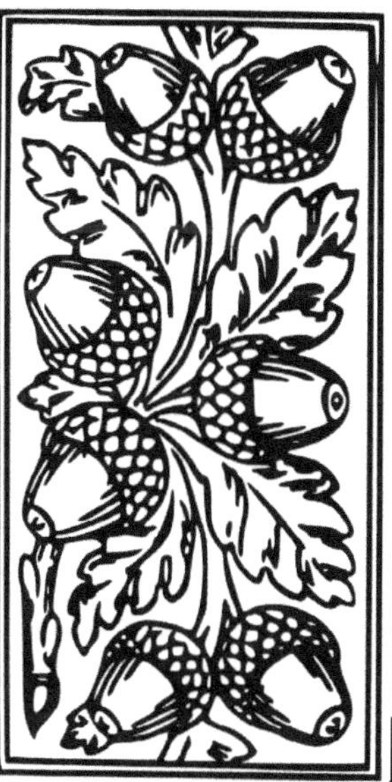
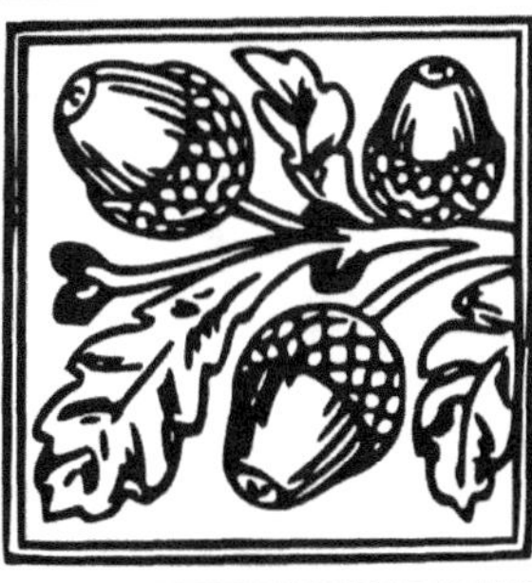

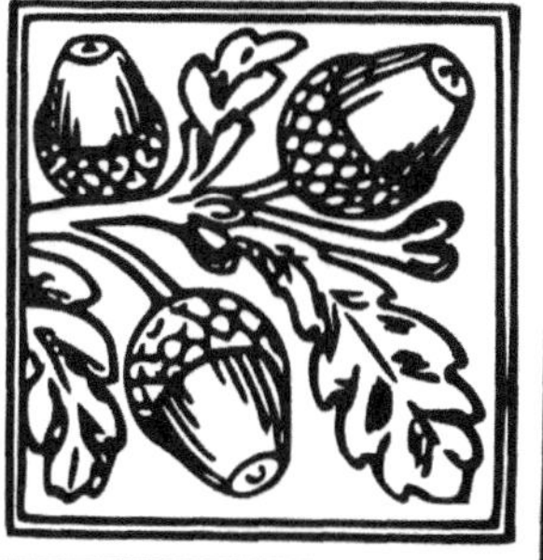

All Scripture is inspired
by God and profitable
for teaching, for reproof,
for correction, and
for training in righteousness.

- 2 Timothy 3:16

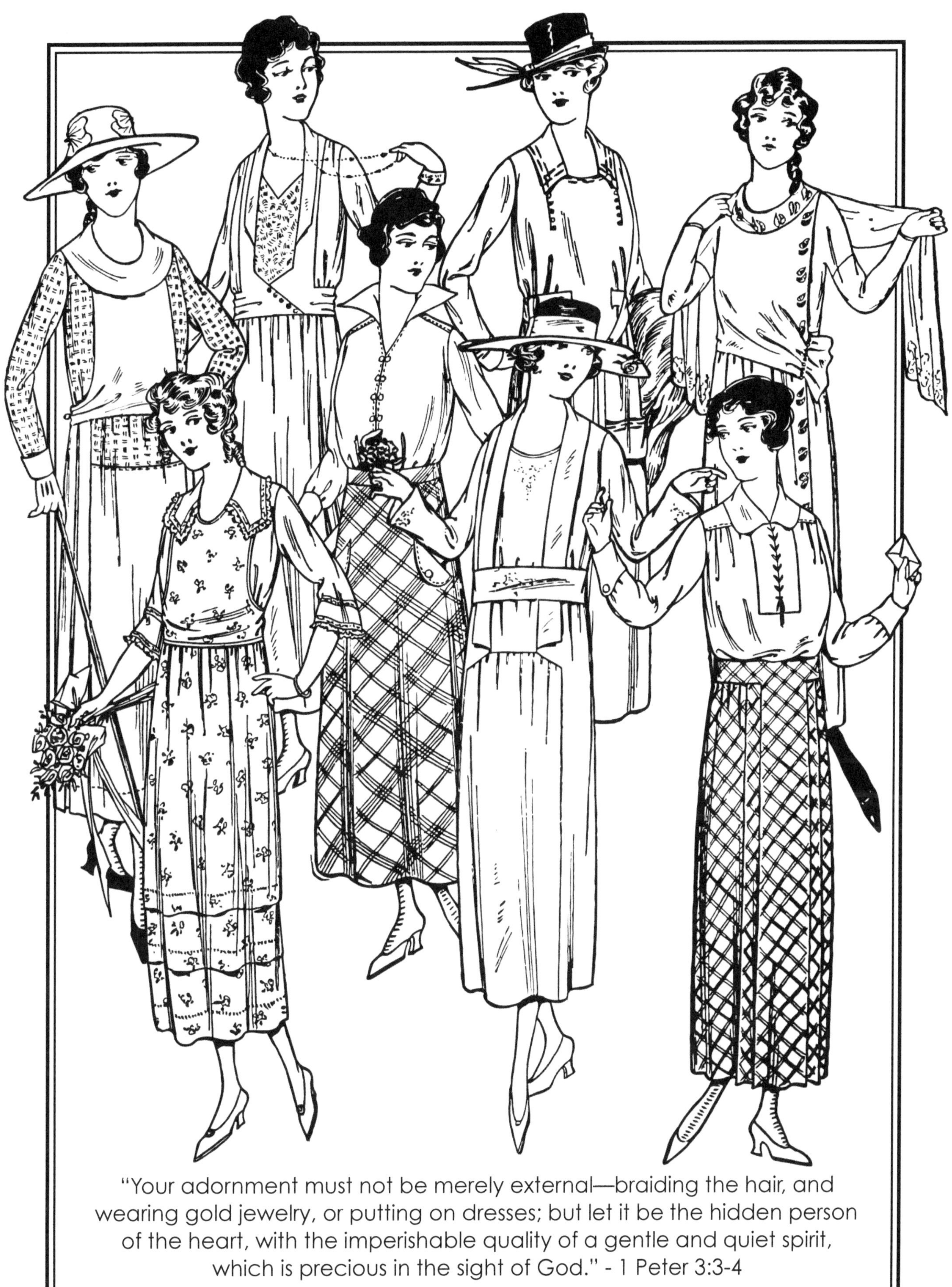

"Your adornment must not be merely external—braiding the hair, and wearing gold jewelry, or putting on dresses; but let it be the hidden person of the heart, with the imperishable quality of a gentle and quiet spirit, which is precious in the sight of God." - 1 Peter 3:3-4

All Scripture is inspired
by God and profitable
for teaching, for reproof,
for correction, and
for training in righteousness.

- 2 Timothy 3:16

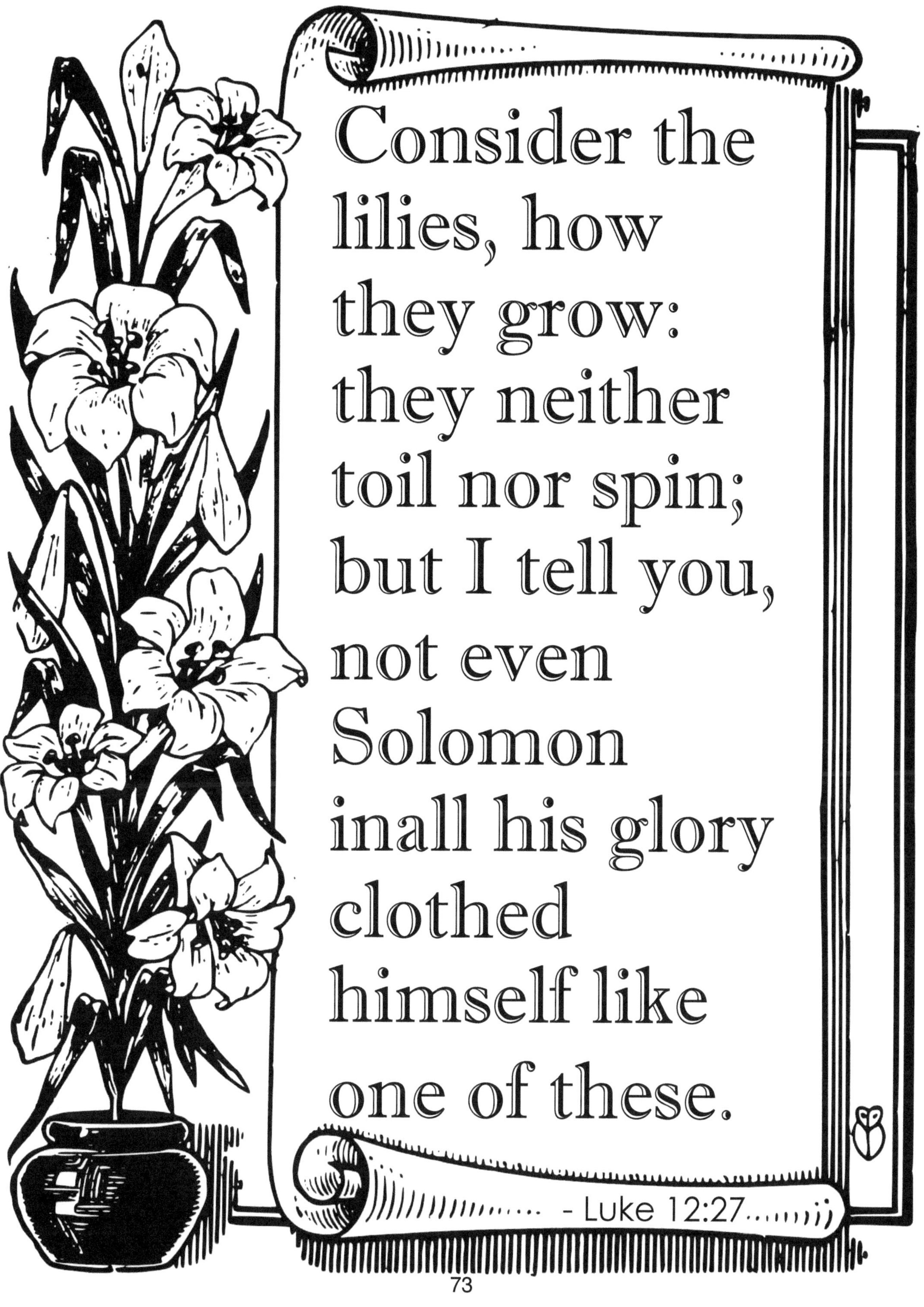
Consider the
lilies, how
they grow:
they neither
toil nor spin;
but I tell you,
not even
Solomon
inall his glory
clothed
himself like
one of these.
- Luke 12:27

All Scripture is inspired
by God and profitable
for teaching, for reproof,
for correction, and
for training in righteousness.

- 2 Timothy 3:16

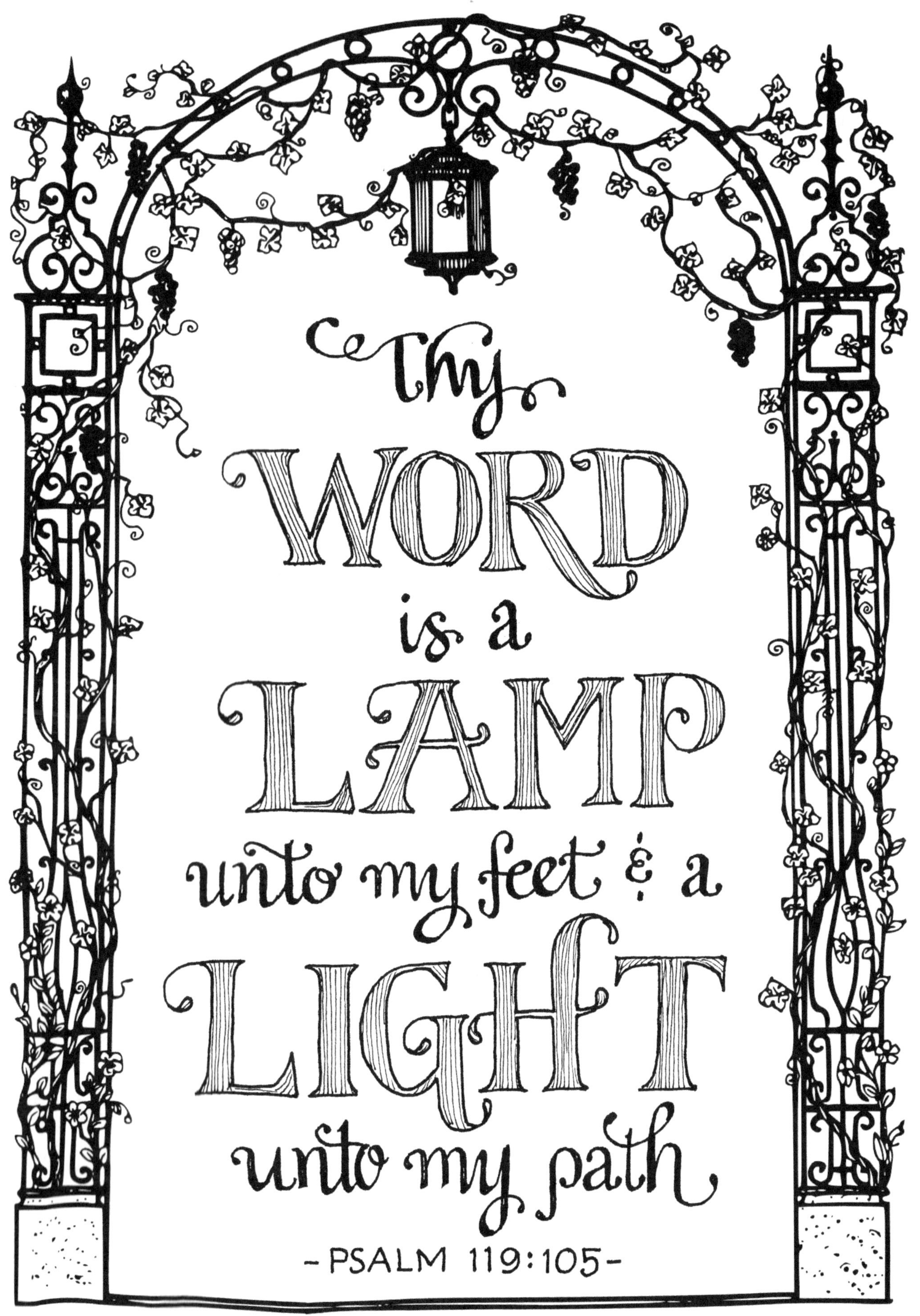
Thy
WORD
is a
LAMP
unto my feet & a
LIGHT
unto my path
-PSALM 119:105-

All Scripture is inspired
by God and profitable
for teaching, for reproof,
for correction, and
for training in righteousness.

- 2 Timothy 3:16

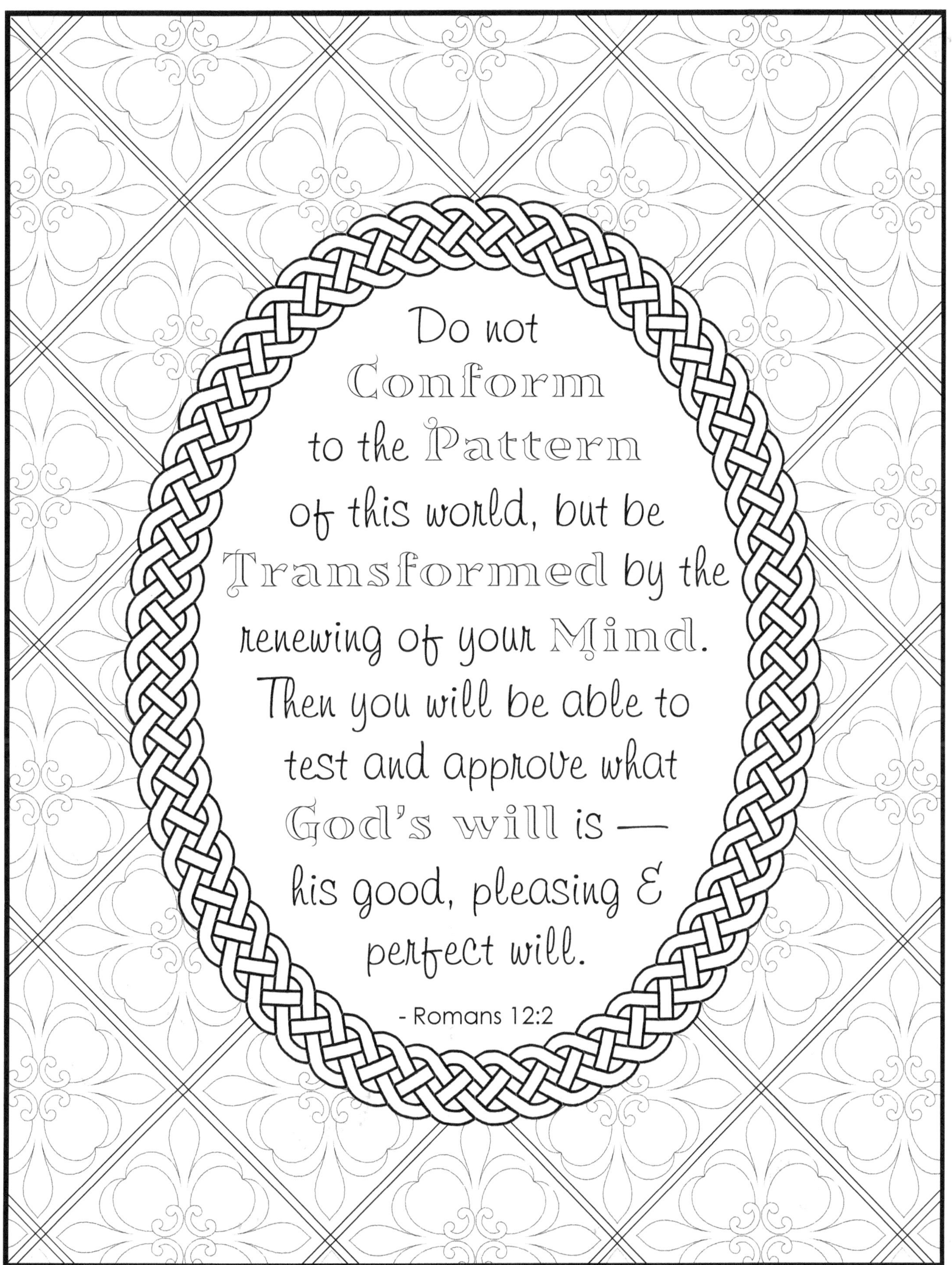
Do not
Conform
to the Pattern
of this world, but be
Transformed by the
renewing of your Mind.
Then you will be able to
test and approve what
God's will is —
his good, pleasing &
perfect will.
- Romans 12:2

All Scripture is inspired
by God and profitable
for teaching, for reproof,
for correction, and
for training in righteousness.

- 2 Timothy 3:16 -

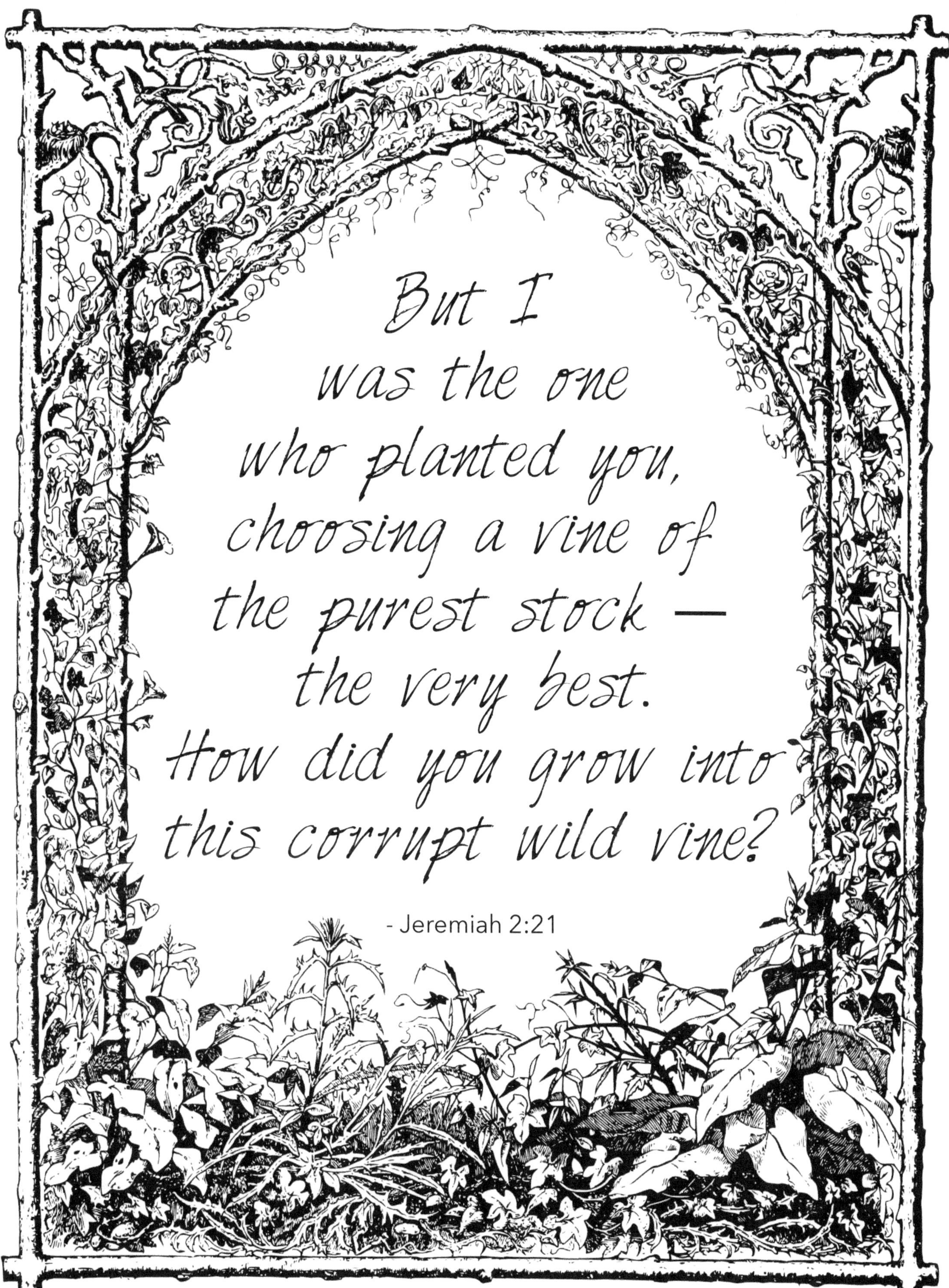
But I
was the one
who planted you,
choosing a vine of
the purest stock —
the very best.
How did you grow into
this corrupt wild vine?
- Jeremiah 2:21

All Scripture is inspired
by God and profitable
for teaching, for reproof,
for correction, and
for training in righteousness.

- 2 Timothy 3:16

My Brethren,
Count it all JOY
when you fall into various
TRIALS
knowing that the testing of
YOUR FAITH
WORKETH Patience unto you.

James 1:2-3

All Scripture is inspired
by God and profitable
for teaching, for reproof,
for correction, and
for training in righteousness.

- 2 Timothy 3:16

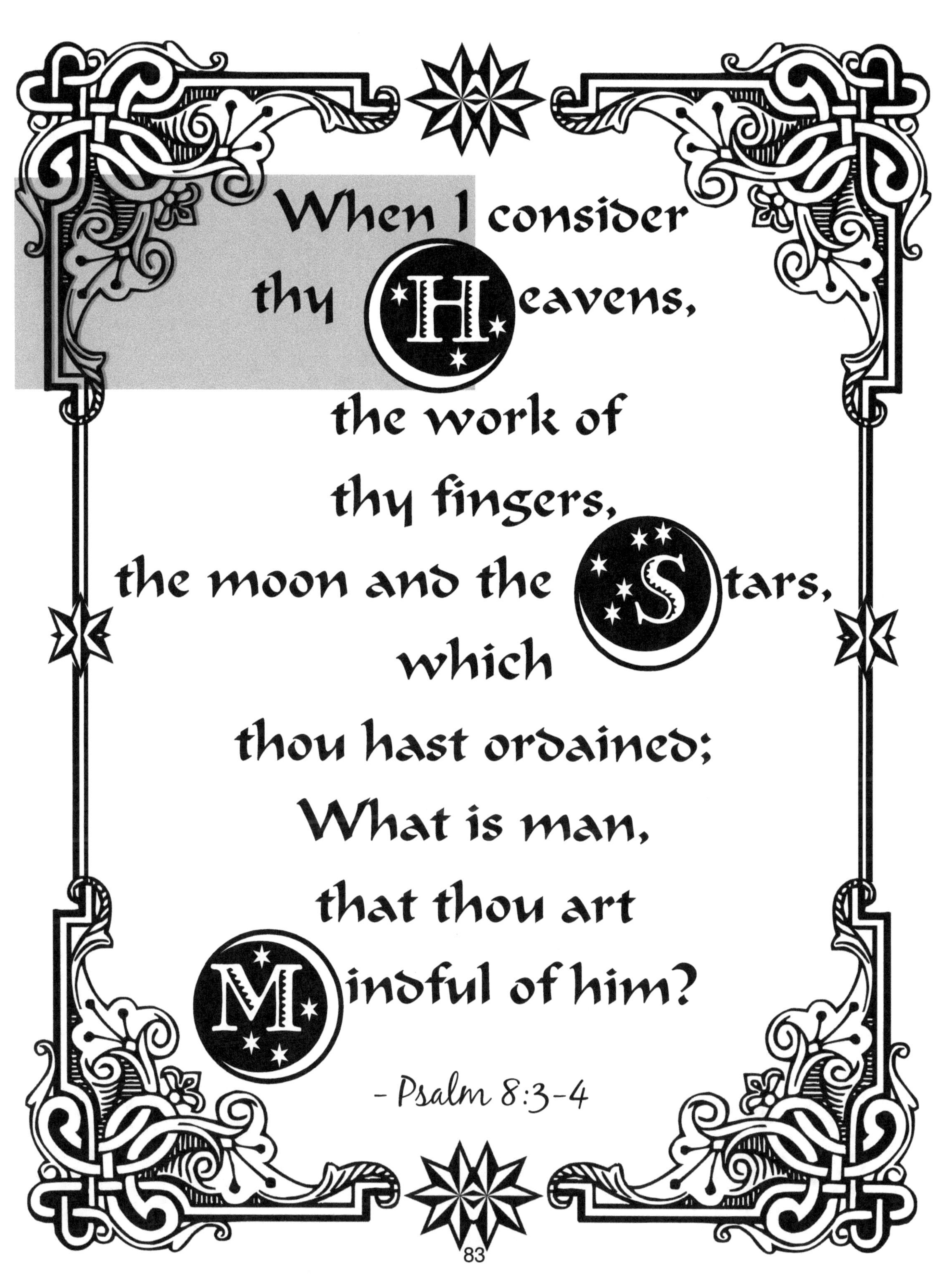
When I consider
thy Heavens,
the work of
thy fingers,
the moon and the Stars,
which
thou hast ordained;
What is man,
that thou art
Mindful of him?
- Psalm 8:3-4

All Scripture is inspired
by God and profitable
for teaching, for reproof,
for correction, and
for training in righteousness.

- 2 Timothy 3:16

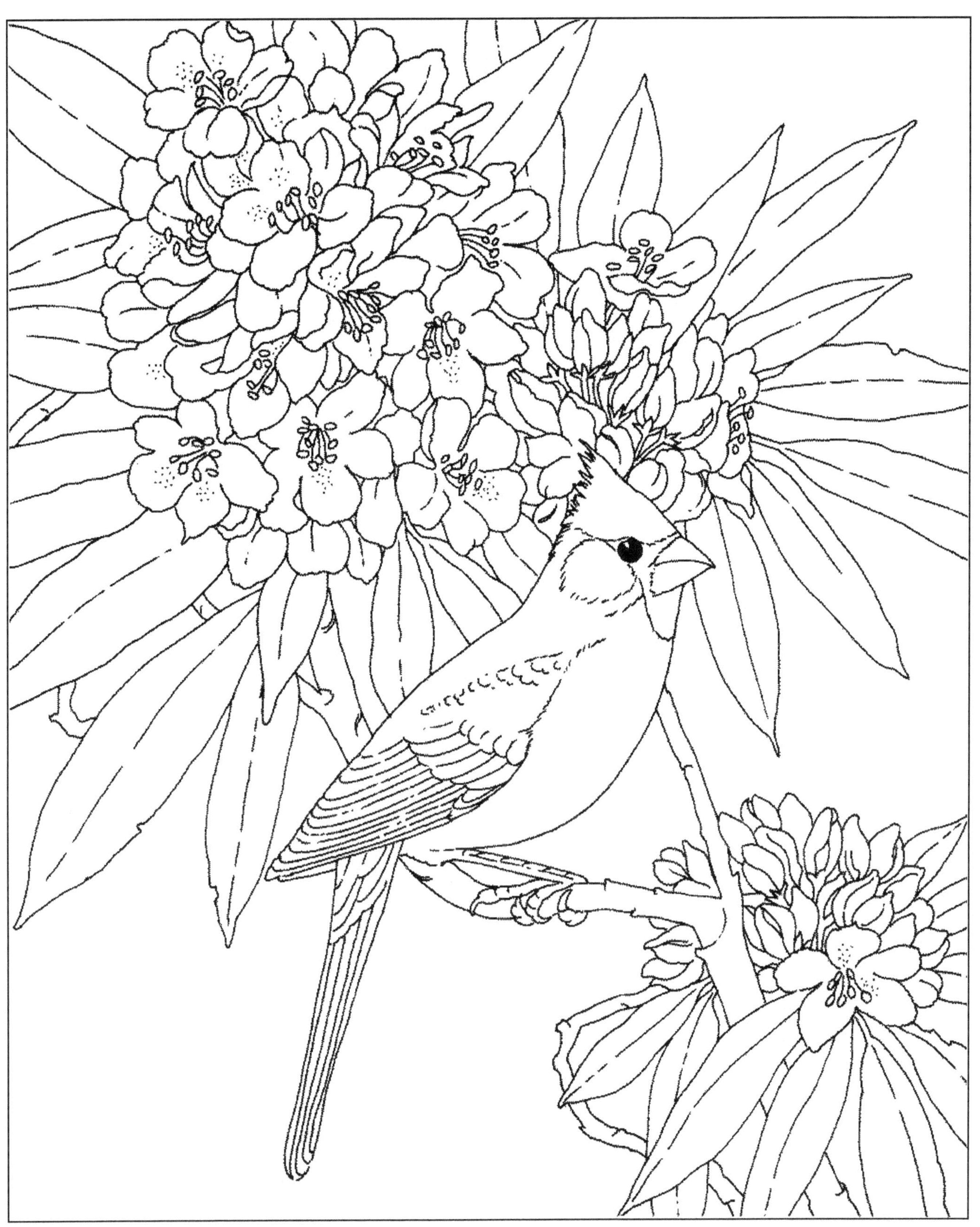

We escaped like a bird from a hunter's trap.
The trap is broken, and we are free! – Psalm 124:7

All Scripture is inspired
by God and profitable
for teaching, for reproof,
for correction, and
for training in righteousness.

- 2 Timothy 3:16

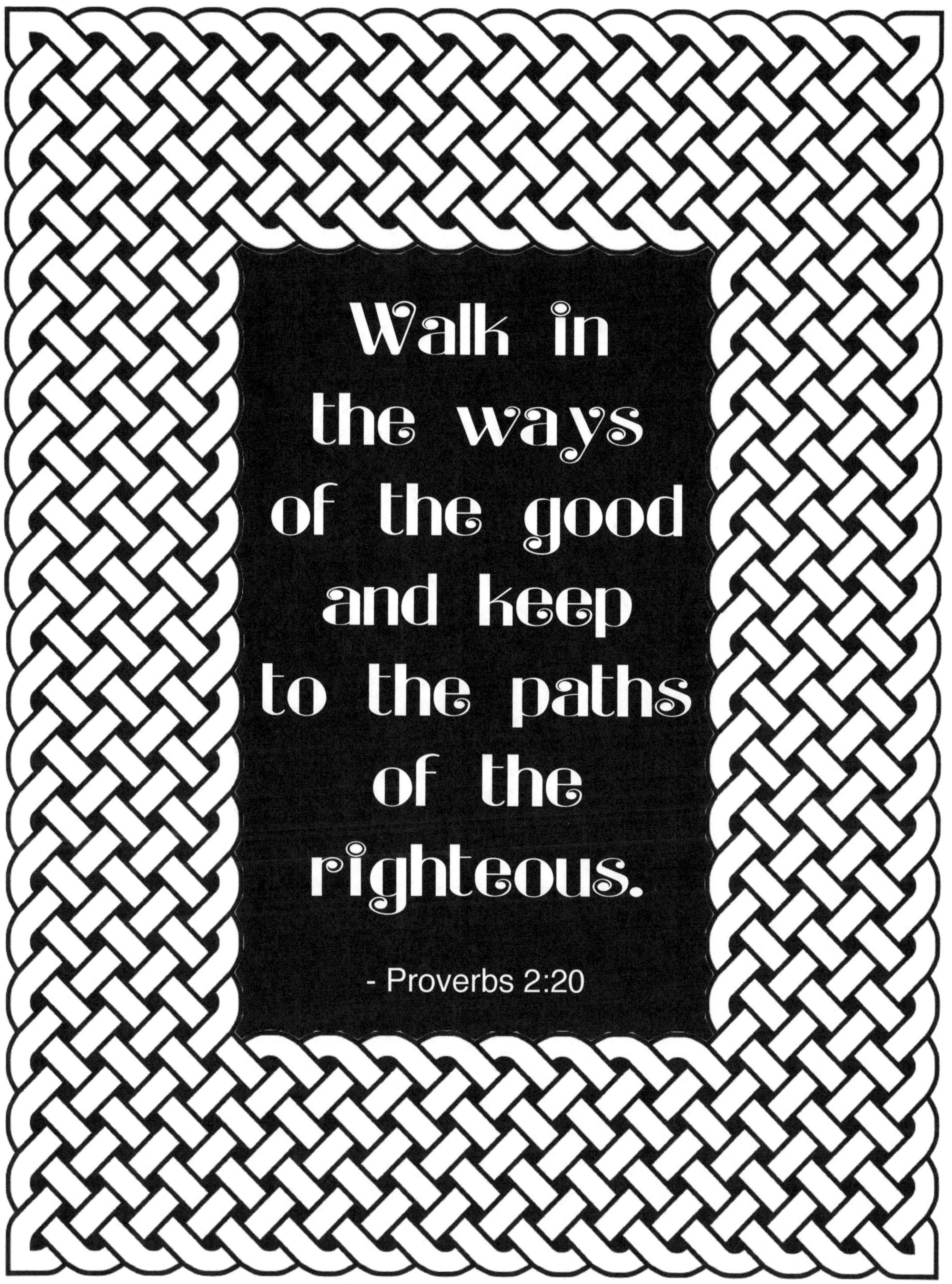
Walk in
the ways
of the good
and keep
to the paths
of the
righteous.
- Proverbs 2:20

All Scripture is inspired
by God and profitable
for teaching, for reproof,
for correction, and
for training in righteousness.

- 2 Timothy 3:16

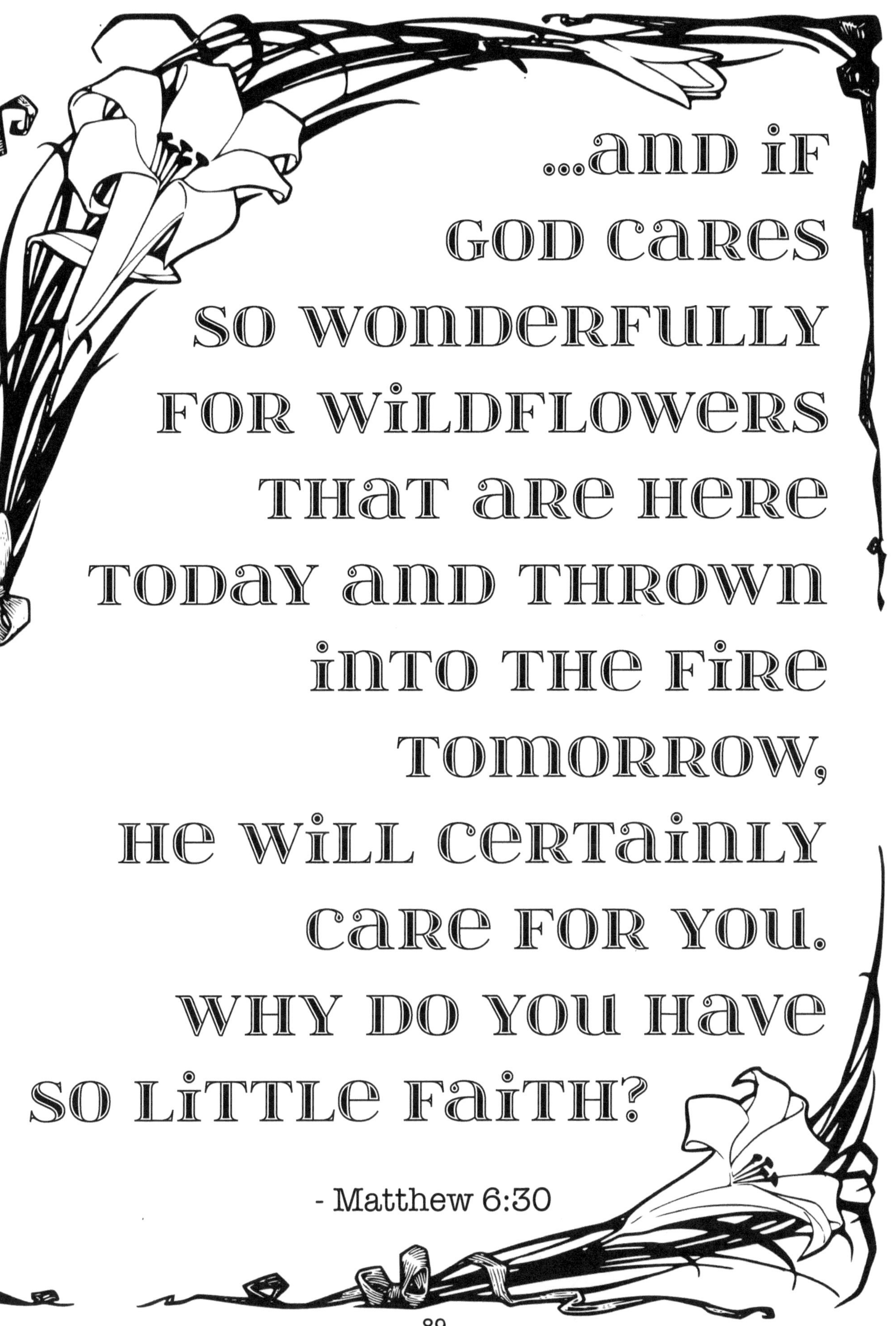

...and if God cares so wonderfully for wildflowers that are here today and thrown into the fire tomorrow, he will certainly care for you. Why do you have so little faith?

- Matthew 6:30

All Scripture is inspired
by God and profitable
for teaching, for reproof,
for correction, and
for training in righteousness.

- 2 Timothy 3:16

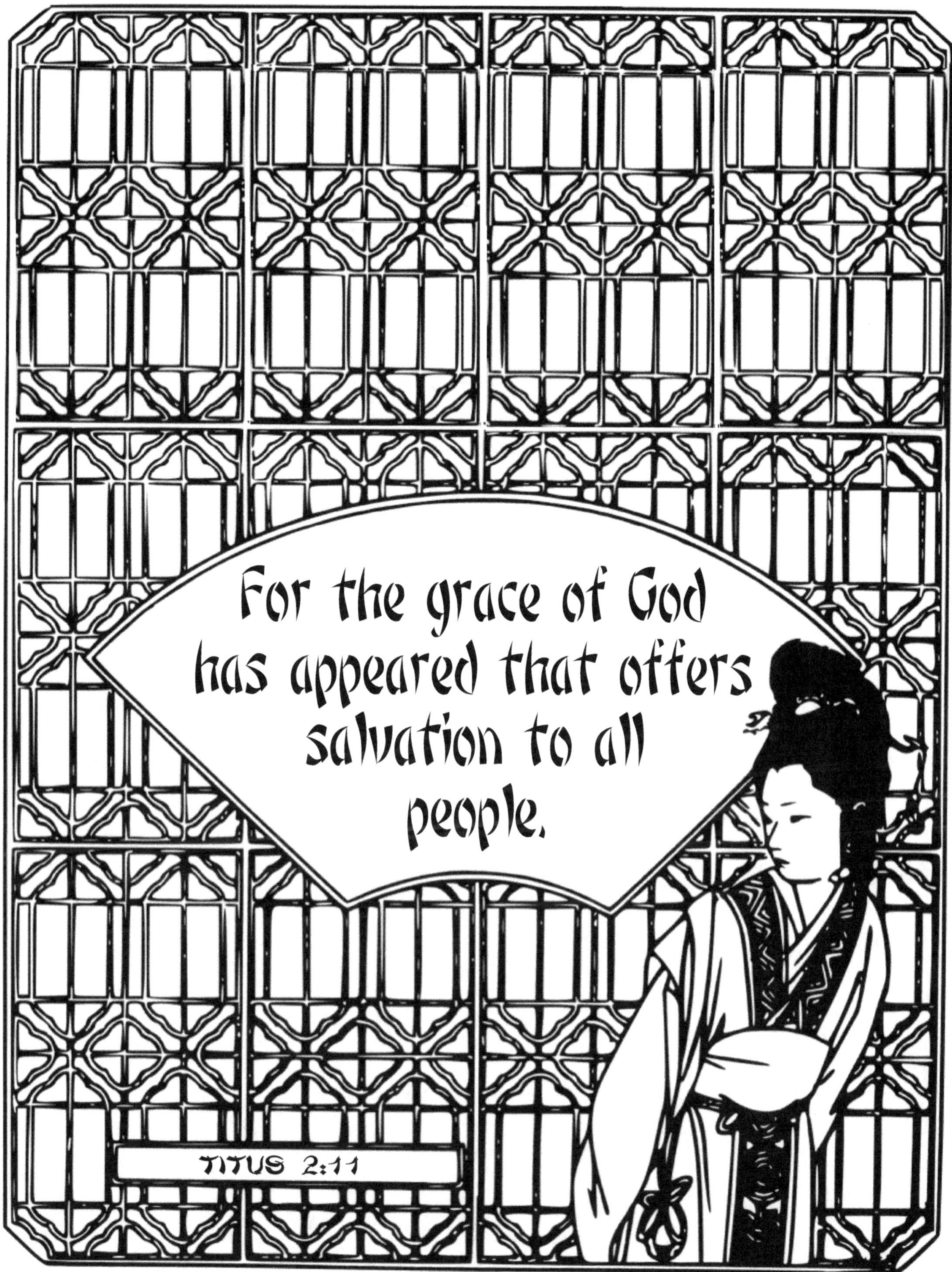
For the grace of God
has appeared that offers
salvation to all
people.
TITUS 2:11

All Scripture is inspired
by God and profitable
for teaching, for reproof,
for correction, and
for training in righteousness.

- 2 Timothy 3:16

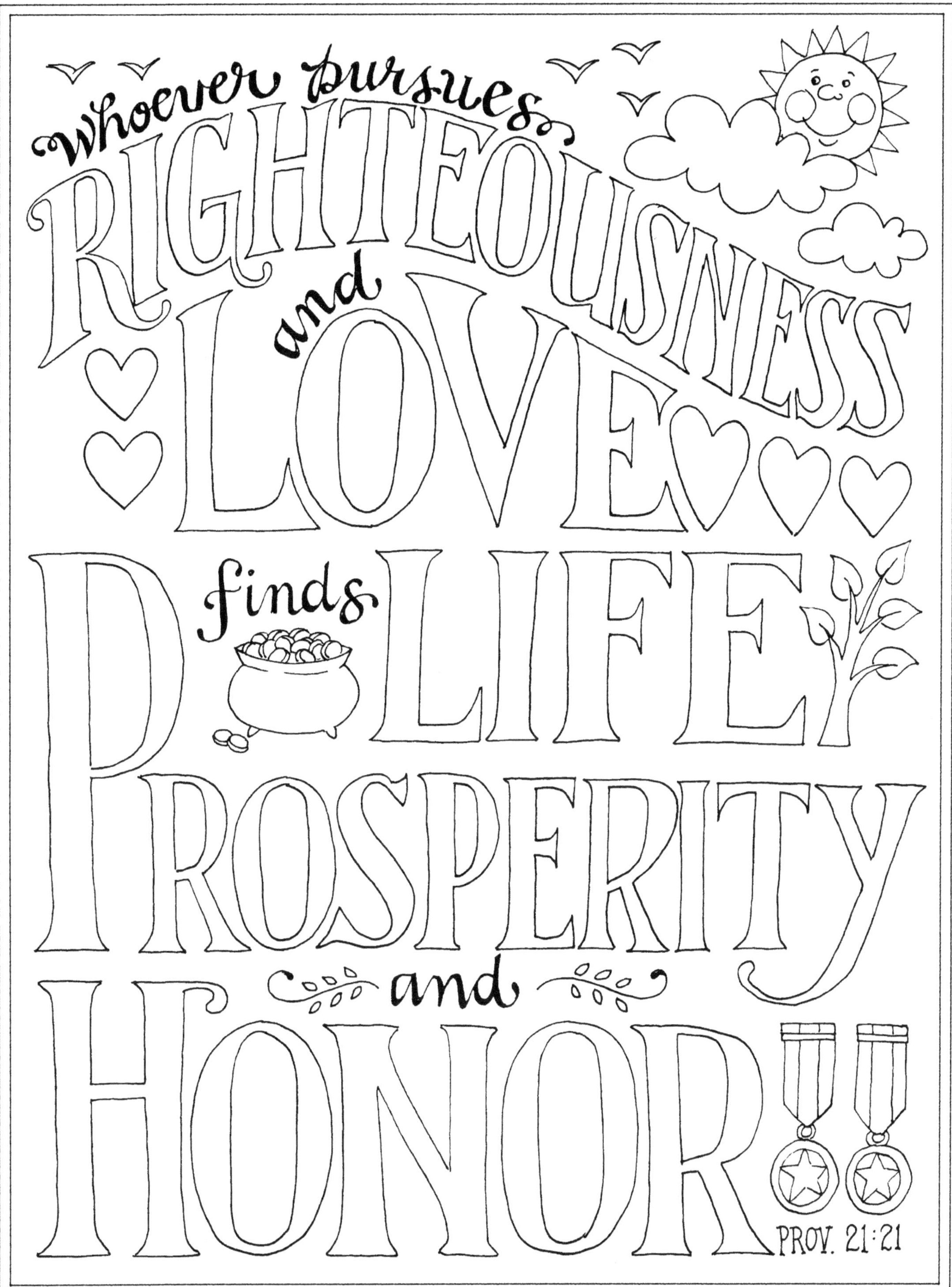
whoever pursues
RIGHTEOUSNESS
and
LOVE
finds
LIFE
PROSPERITY
and
HONOR!!
PROV. 21:21

All Scripture is inspired
by God and profitable
for teaching, for reproof,
for correction, and
for training in righteousness.

– 2 Timothy 3:16

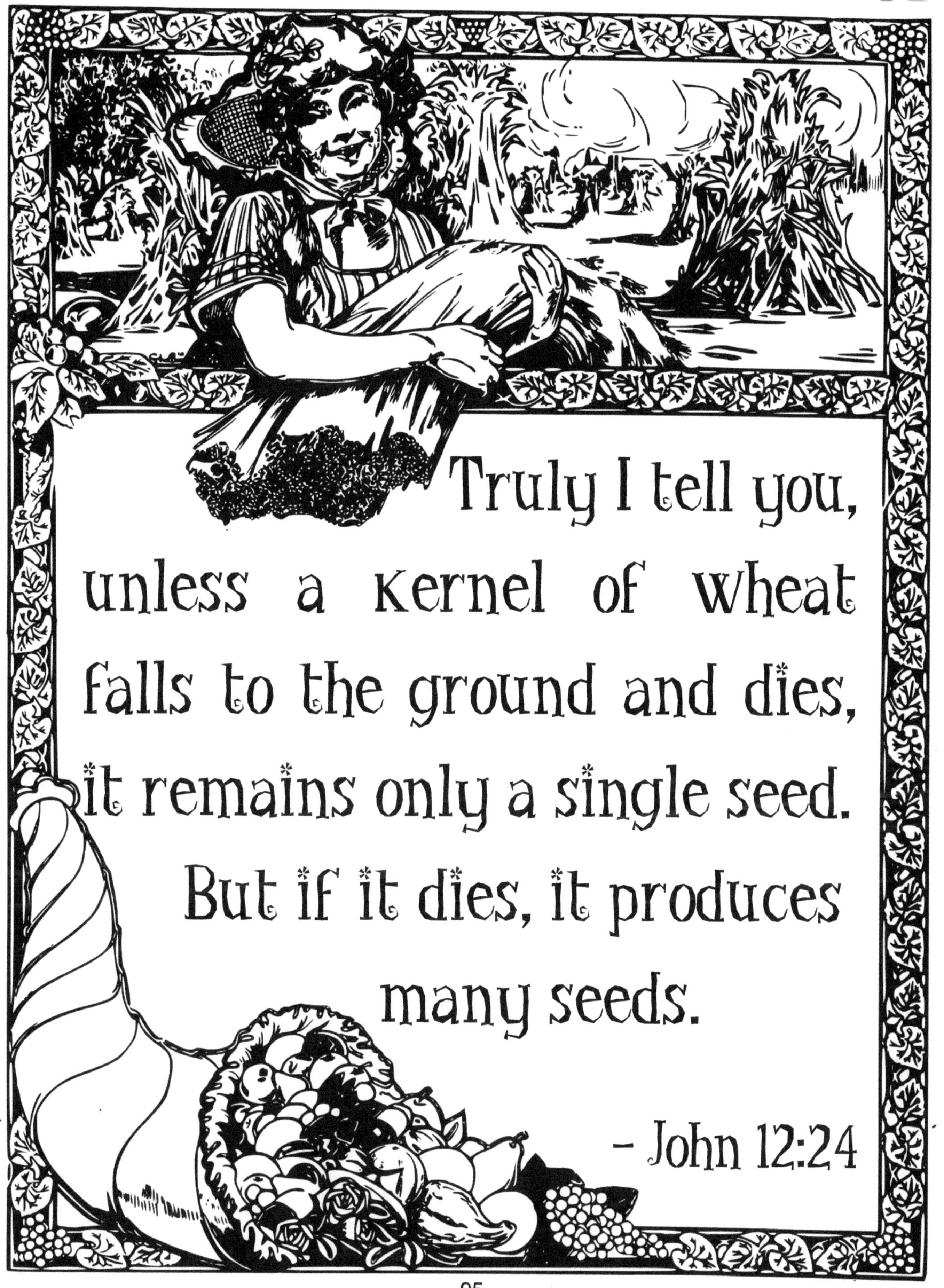
Truly I tell you,
unless a kernel of wheat
falls to the ground and dies,
it remains only a single seed.
But if it dies, it produces
many seeds.
- John 12:24

All Scripture is inspired
by God and profitable
for teaching, for reproof,
for correction, and
for training in righteousness.

- 2 Timothy 3:16

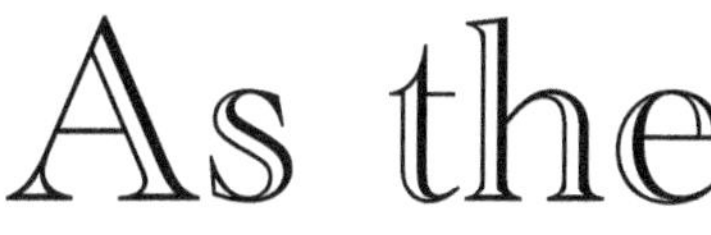

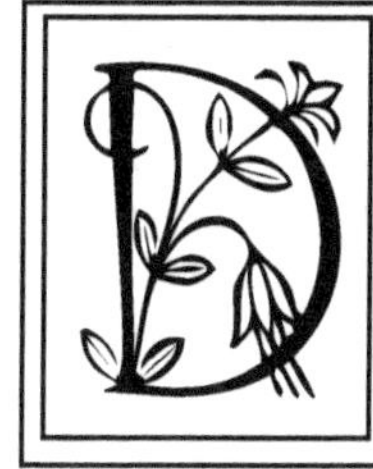

As the Deer pants
for the water brooks,

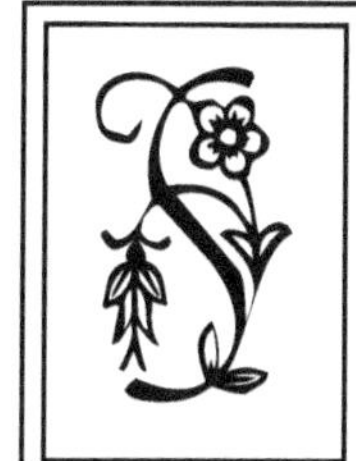

So my soul
pants for You,
O God.

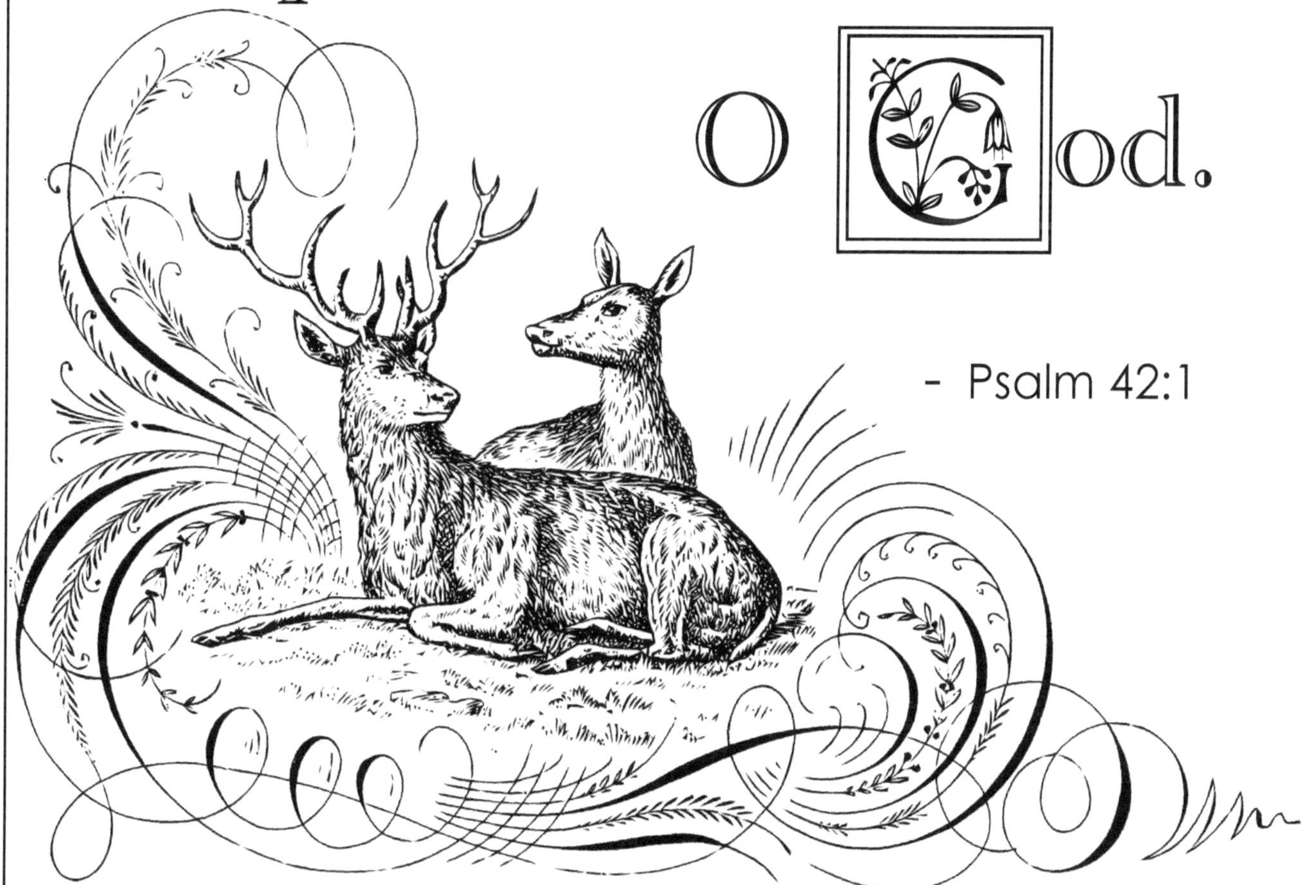

- Psalm 42:1

All Scripture is inspired
by God and profitable
for teaching, for reproof,
for correction, and
for training in righteousness.

- 2 Timothy 3:16

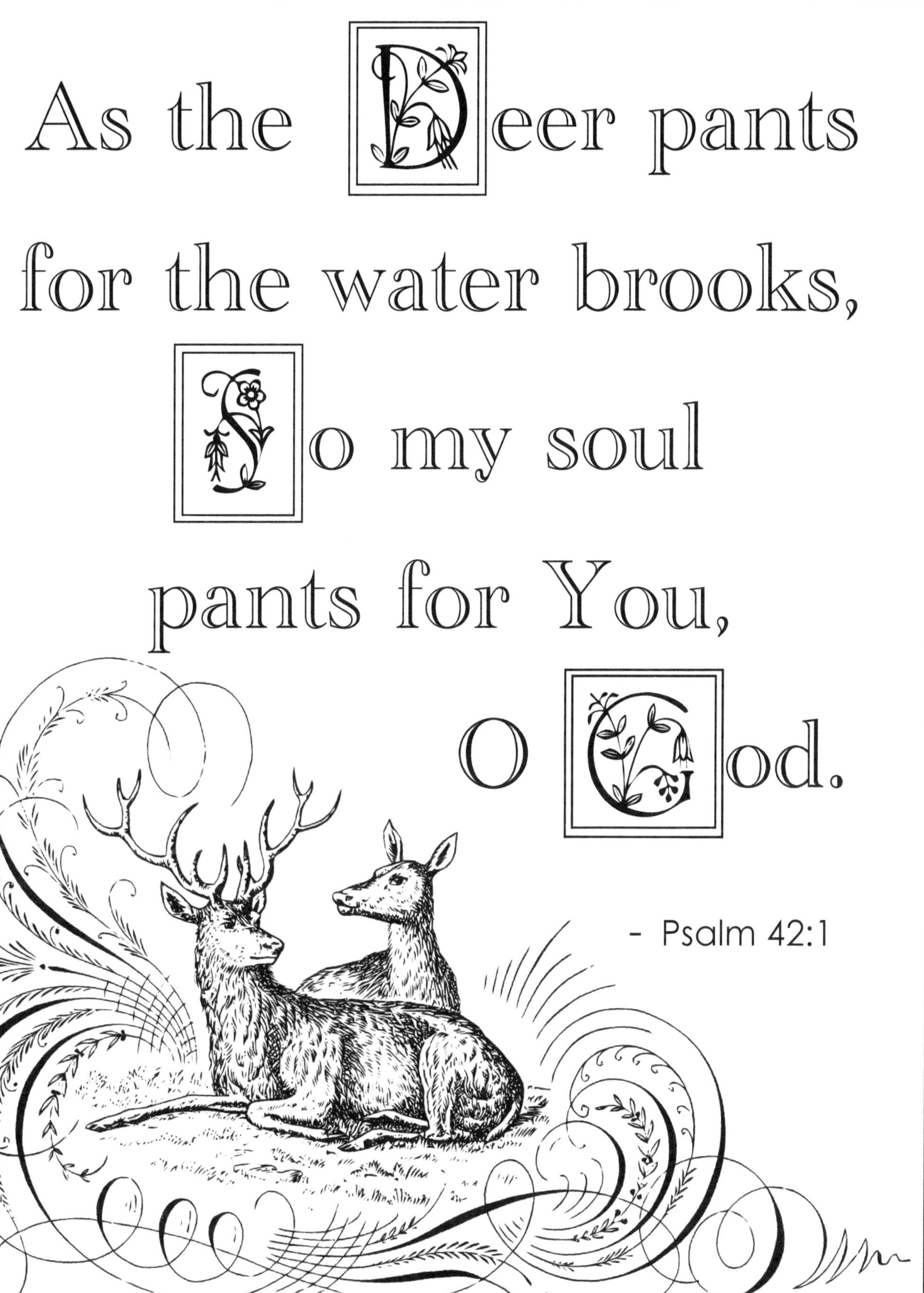
As the Deer pants
for the water brooks,
So my soul
pants for You,
O God.
- Psalm 42:1

All Scripture is inspired
by God and profitable
for teaching, for reproof,
for correction, and
for training in righteousness.

- 2 Timothy 3:16

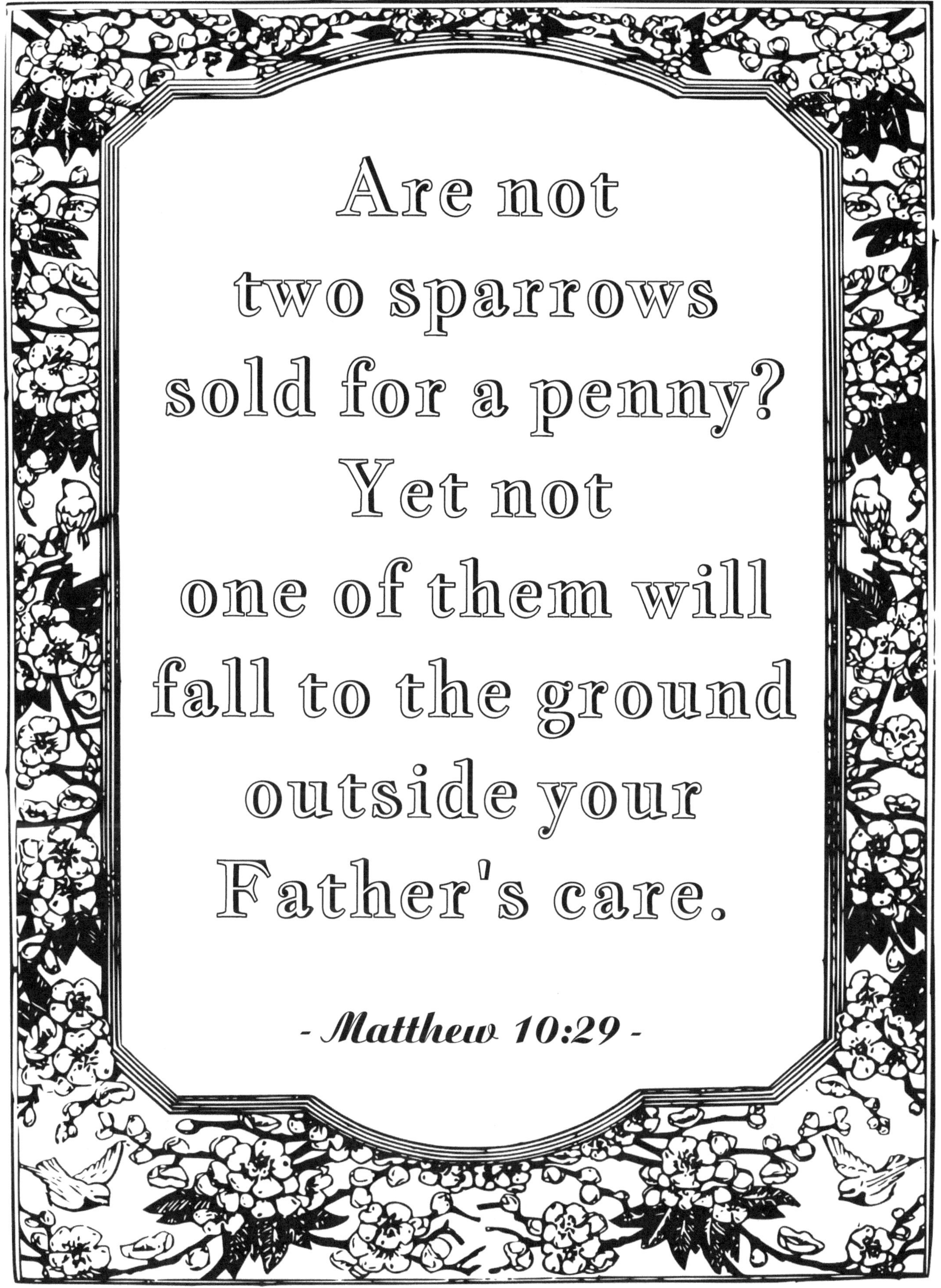
Are not
two sparrows
sold for a penny?
Yet not
one of them will
fall to the ground
outside your
Father's care.
- Matthew 10:29 -

More books from Jennifer Flanders:

25 Ways to Communicate Respect to Your Husband

Balance: The Art of Minding What Matters Most

Get Up & Go: Fun Ideas for Getting Fit as a Family

And if you enjoy writing as well as coloring, you'll want to check out our new devotional journals. With over 200 pages of Scripture-based artwork, word studies & writing prompts, they combine the best of both worlds:

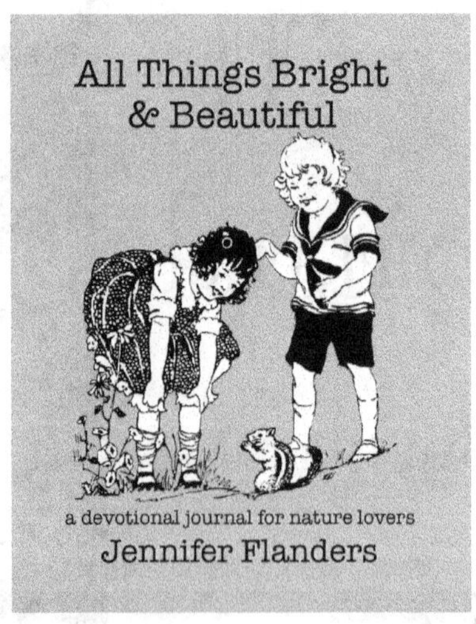

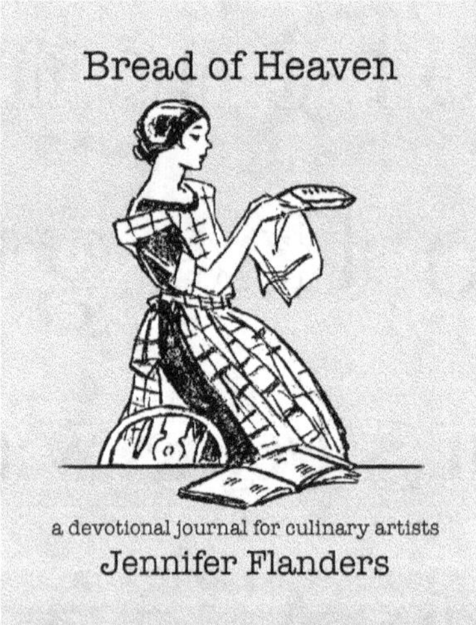

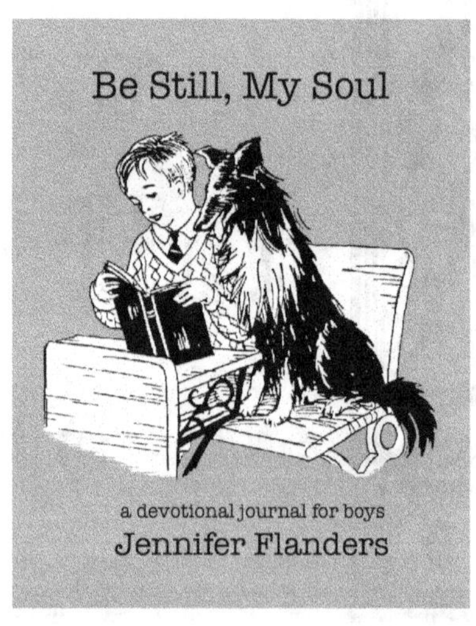

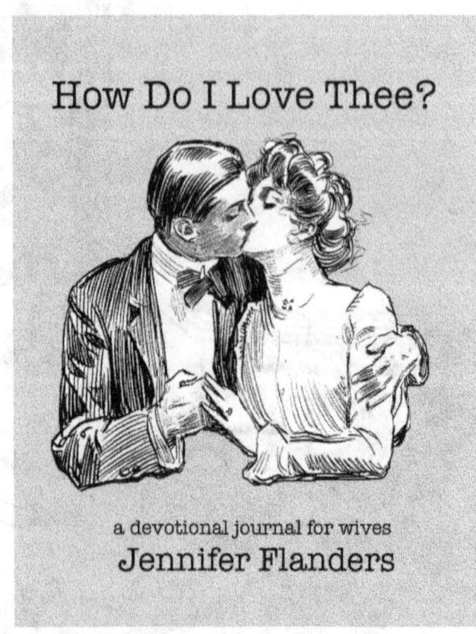

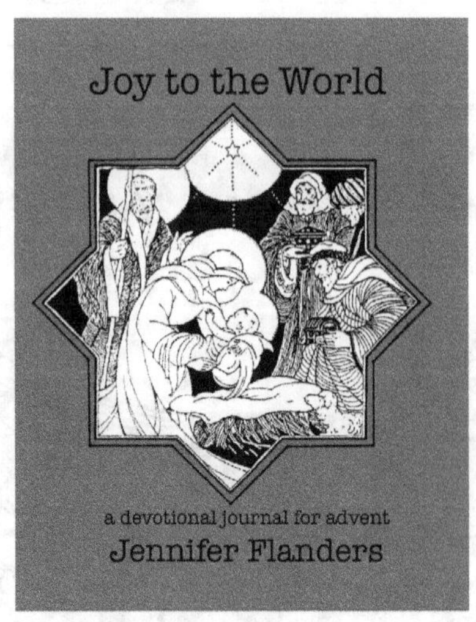

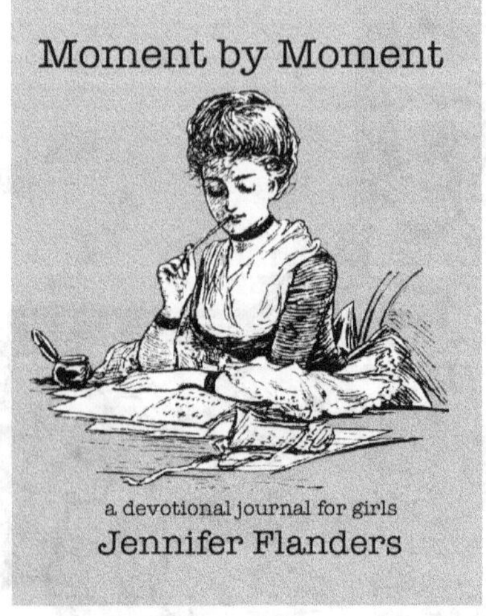

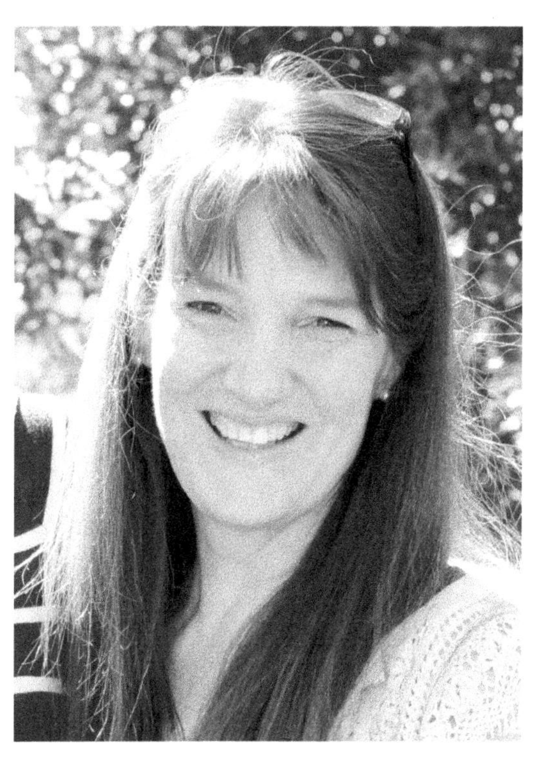

About the Artist:

Jennifer Flanders has been drawing since she was old enough to hold a pencil. She has spent half a century honing her craft and sincerely hopes you will enjoy the fruit of her labor in the form of this coloring book.

Although Jennifer loves art in all its various forms, her greatest and most challenging creative endeavor has been raising (and homeschooling) the twelve children she and her husband have been blessed with since their marriage in 1987.

Many of her children share her affinity for doodling and have been drawing since they were old enough to hold a pencil.

You can read more from Jennifer (& find lots of downloadable coloring pages & other free printable goodies) by visiting her family website:

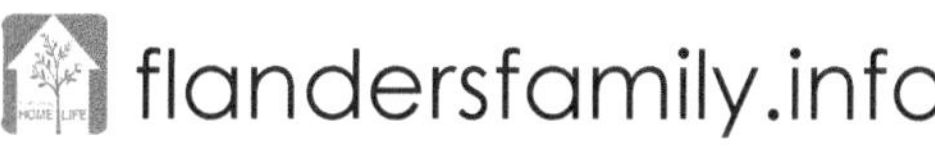

or by connecting with her online through social media or her personal blog:

TheFlandersFamily

flanders_family

flanders_family

flandersfamily

lovinglifeathome.com

Love.Your.Husband.Yourself

www.ingramcontent.com/pod-product-compliance
Lightning Source LLC
LaVergne TN
LVHW080924110826
845155LV00039B/200

* 9 7 8 1 9 3 8 9 4 5 1 9 9 *